JESUS CHRIST SUPERSTAR

THE AUTHORISED VERSION

Blessed are
Andrew, Tim, Sarah, Andy, David, Deborah, Jules,
Alan, Tammy, Tom, Liz, Sandra, Laurie,
Jim, Nessie, Terry, Bob, Mick and Andy

All lyrics and music
© Copyright by Leeds Music Ltd. 1970
© Copyright 'Herod's Song' by Norrie Paramour Ltd. 1970

Colour Photos by Jay Thompson-Camera Press

IBM Typesetting by West Two

Cover and colour illustrations printed by
Cripplegate Printing Company Ltd.

Made and printed in Great Britain by
C. Nicholls & Company Ltd., The Philips Park Press, Manchester

Acknowledgement is gratefully given to the following for the use of their material:

The Evening Standard; Green Lantern Comics; Hodder & Stoughton Ltd;
The Hollywood Reporter; Jesus Comics – The Rip Off Press; Los Angeles
Free Press; The Los Angeles Times; The New York Daily News; The New Yorker;
The New York Times; Paradine Productions; Rock Magazine; Rolling Stone;
The Sunday Mirror; 'Time' – The Weekly News Magazine; Times Newspapers Ltd.;
'Variety'; The Village Voice; Westinghouse Broadcasting Corporation Inc.

CONDITIONS OF SALE

JESUS CHRIST SUPERSTAR
The Authorised Version

Compiled by
Michael Braun

with
Richard Eckford & Peter Stimpson

A Pan Original
PAN BOOKS LTD : LONDON

First published 1972 by Pan Books Ltd.,
33 Tothill Street, London, SW1.

ISBN O 330 23517 6

nd it came to pass that

St. John the Baptist's Birth foretold.

Tim Rice was born on the 10th of November, 1944 in Amersham, Buckinghamshire.

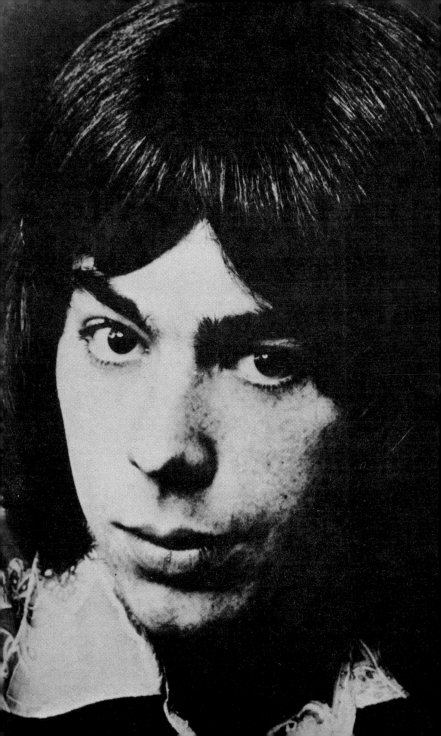

And Andrew Lloyd Webber on
the 22nd of March, 1948 in
London.

And Tim after attending Lancing College, Sussex and the University of Paris became a petrol pump attendant and a law student before joining EMI and the Norrie Paramour Organisation as a record producer.

And Andrew having won a Queens Scholarship to Westminster School and a History Exhibition to Magdelen College, Oxford, left to study music at the Royal College of Music.

11 Gunter Grove

LONDON, S.W. 10

April 21 1965

Dear Andrew,

    I have been told that you "were looking for a 'with-it'
writer" of lyrics for your songs, and as I have been writing
pop songs for a short while now and particularly enjoy writing
the lyrics I wondered if you considered it worth your while
meeting me. I may fall far short of your requirements, but
anyway it would be interesting to meet up--I hope! Would you
be able to get in touch with me shortly, either at FLA 1822
in the evenings, or at WEL 2261 in the daytime (Pettit and
Westlake, solicitors are the owners of the latter number.)

           Hoping to hear from you,

                Yours,

                Tim Rice

And lo, having met, they wrote a musical based on the life of Doctor Barnado which never got off the ground and then they wrote several songs and finally an oratorio based on the Biblical story of Joseph called 'Joseph and the Amazing Technicolor Dreamcoat,' which was very well received.

And then, in the Year of Our Lord One Thousand, Nine Hundred and Sixty Nine they began to think about a work that would ultimately bring good tidings of great joy.

Presentation in the Temple.

THE
NEW TESTAMENT
OF
JESUS CHRIST
SUPERSTAR

THE GOSPEL ACCORDING TO
TIM AND ANDREW

Tim: The first record of our having had the idea appeared in January '69, so we were very vaguely thinking about it the beginning of '69, but not much before that. Really before 1969 we were hardly in a position to think about doing anything.

1 **Andrew:** I can remember having a very entertaining discussion with the vicar of — what's the church in Queensgate — St. Augustine's Queensgate when I was at the Royal College of Music, in '69 I suppose it was, and he said what a fantastic idea to do a musical on Christ and I said it would be a terrible idea because it would never sell.

2 **Tim:** All we saw Superstar as was one more step up the ladder to eventually making it as a theatrical writing team. You see Andrew had his bursting ambition to be Rishard Rodgers. I sort of vaguely wanted to be Elvis . . . but then Andrew persuaded me to write some lyrics for a musical he wanted to do on Doctor Barnado. By that time I had joined EMI as a serf under the title of management trainee. We had sold the rights to Doctor Barnado for £100 each and for 2 years we waited. Nothing much happened and then in the summer of 1967 we managed to get two songs of ours recorded by Ross Haniman who was the Evening Standard's Girl of the Year. We also were asked by Alan Doggett to write something for the boys at the school where he was then teaching. At the beginning of 1968 we wrote 'Joseph and His Technicolor Dreamcoat' and then at one performance Derek Jewell of The Sunday Times' who happened to have a child at the school wrote this fantastic review. That got it recorded and it was our first really big break. I was still with Norrie Paramour recording Cliff and the Shadows and the Scaffold all of which was remarkably good experience. At the beginning of 1969 we put 'Joseph' on at St. Paul's.

3 **Andrew:** Through this we had met the Dean of St. Paul's and in May 1969 we went to him to discuss writing a musical about Christ. He said we should do what we liked so we wrote the single because we were still trying to deal very gingerly with the whole subject. By the way he was the only person who anticipated a controversy when he told us we might be accused of anti-Semitism, but we never thought of it again because obviously it isn't anti-Semitic.

4 **Tim:** I suppose I was fascinated particularly by Judas Iscariot and, corny though it may sound, the Dylan song 'With God on Our Side' which has that all time great lyric "I can't think for you, you'll have to decide, did Judas Iscariot have God on his side." That really made me think well there's a fantastic story here and I've always had since I was about ten, an ambition to one day write a play about either Pilate or Judas and bring Christ in as an incidental character, although in 'Superstar' Christ is much more than an incidental character. . . . We were thinking much more on lines of theatre — we only did it on record in the first place purely because we wanted to use the record as a demonstration disc and nothing more really to impress some theatrical man to put it on.

5 **Andrew:** I had written to Sefton Myers because he had managed a pop star I knew called David Ballantine. I wanted to get him to back an idea of mine for setting up a museum for pop music in London with things like Elvis' guitar. I remember our first meeting because Sefton was very busy but David Land was there and I remember I thought 'What an imposing man.' Well anyway, what happened was that for one reason or the other they didn't want to do the museum but they had heard 'Joseph' and they decided to back us.

6 **Tim:** At about the time we got involved with David and Sefton we started thinking about what we were going to do next. JC was only one of the projects that we talked about but I must say we wanted to have something with a strong central character and the more that people told us it was OK especially clergymen, the more we went off it, ironic as that might sound. Anyway, we then wrote 'Come Back Richard' about Richard the Lionheart which was an enormous flop and we began thinking again.

7 **Andrew:** I had been trying to think up a tune for a title song and then one night as I was walking down the Fulham

FROST: Which comes first of the two—well how was Jesus Chr **Superstar first started? TIM: In the writing-wise, in sort of three stag** **first together we work out, as it were, the plot, you know, and who w** **be doing what in each scene and then Andrew will write the mu**

The Epiphany.

Road to a restaurant called Carlo's Place I started getting a melody and when I got to the restaurant I wrote it down on a napkin. There were several suggestions for subjects — Alan Doggett said it should be about the Daily Mail Air Race — but we knew it was perfect for 'Superstar'.

8 Tim: . . . I remember very clearly writing the lyrics just before Sunday lunch at home, you know my parents' home in Hatfield, and I had this tune, this chorus was one that Andrew had had for 2 or 3 months, da da da and you know we just wanted a really moving rhythm track chunk chunk chunk and umm I wrote these words anyway and again everybody says how did the word 'Superstar' come but it really — I just thought well I'd written this chorus which originally was 'Jesus Christ, Jesus Christ' 4 times over I thought 'that's rather boring you know can I call him something and 'Superstar' scanned so I put it in. I hadn't even heard of Warhol then, it was a word that I'd heard once or twice used in Melody Maker or something you know it was just a word to describe a really — now of course it's devalued you know 'bass guitarist with the Trogs is a Superstar' but at that time Eric Clapton, John Lennon, Mick Jagger that was about it, were called Superstars.' I think Tom Jones at that time was having adverts "The world's No. one superstar". We then needed someone to sing it. One of the people who I was forced to record at EMI was Murray Head. Nobody would talk to him because he had a contract to record three songs and he had recorded two which had flopped. I got him and the Grease Band together because David had brought us to MCA through his friendship with Cyril Simons who became our publisher and commissioned the work. Finally, in October 1969 we recorded the single, on 8 track at Olympia Studios.

9 Andrew: And I must say I'm still very proud of the orchestral sound which for a single was pretty incredible. It cost a small fortune for a single and I still have memos saying we were off our heads spending that money on a single, but Brian Brolly of MCA backed us all the way.

10 Tim: Anyway the single came out in November 1969 when it was originally called "Jesus Christ." Then we were going to call it "I only want to know" because we

thought if we call it "Jesus Christ" we've had it. Although I notice that Cliff has made a record called "Jesus". Then we decided to call it "Superstar". It lurched out and got incredibly good reactions and fairly good airplay and everybody said it was bound to be a hit, it can't miss and then it didn't make it and we just couldn't believe it but just when we had just about given up and said "right back to the drawing board, lets do one on Robin Hood," it took off in Australia, Belgium, Holland and made a big impact in America where it was a big FM hit and sold 100,000 copies.

11 Andrew: At that point Brian Brolly at MCA told us we could go ahead on the album and after a few discussions David and Sefton agreed.

12 Tim: We then had to write the rest of the opera which at that point was just a sort of outline. Andrew had a few tunes and I had an idea of the plot.

13 Andrew: We did this in about five or six days I suppose. We went to the Stoke Edith House Hotel, Stoke Edith, Herefordshire. This was the week before Christmas in 1969.

14 Tim: The single had just come out and was getting some airplay so we went down to the hotel and went for walks and watched Tom and Jerry on television.

15 Andrew: We really did write a lot though. We wrote 'Heaven on their Minds', 'Everything's all right', really all the third and fourth sides were written there.

16 Tim: The song I had the most difficulty with, funnily enough, was 'I Don't Know How to Love Him.' Patter songs like 'King Herod' are relatively easy. It's the spare and simple lyrics that are always the most difficult to write.

17 Andrew: The most unusual thing at least for me was that practically everything except the old tune that we eventually used for 'Herods Song' was expressly written for 'Superstar' after we got the commission instead of using things that we had already done for something else. Even so, I did re-write a lot, for instance the middle part of "Gethsemane" was practically the last thing I did because I felt the thing I had originally just wasn't right. At the end I think what we had musically was about half rock music and the other half both classical and show music. As for the lyrics may I say

owing roughly what it's going to be about, for example, he will know a love song or it's an up-tempo thing or it's a trial scene, then I will write the lyrics to the music, but basically it's plot—music—lyrics. ANDREW: Sometimes, if there's plot, if there's a lot of plot, Tim sort

Flight into Egypt.

that they are unusually literate for pop music.

18 Tim: They're very un-vague if that's the right word. Most pop writers with the exception of people like Ray Davies, I mean people like Dylan and Paul Simon write stuff that is deliberately unclear. I mean look at "Desolation Row" and "American Pie" which are great but can be interpreted in many different ways. I mean my stuff is really much more dramatic which is why we're better in the theatre. The average rock reviewer looks for deeper meanings but when I write a love song that's what it is, a love song. Some lines such as "To conquer death you only have to die" from Pilate's Dream Sequence which is my own favourite line seem very clear on the surface but there is a lot more to them and people just miss that completely. I'd like to have that on my grave "To conquer death you only have to die" that's the best line in the whole show I think.

19 Tim: In any case we had to find Christ which was a drama in itself with rumours of John Lennon playing the role flying about and then I remember I was up all one night making dog noises on a looped tape for the Temple scene. We were recording with the same mob as did the single like Pete Robinson, Chris Mercer and the Grease Band lads with Alan O'Duffy as our irreplaceable engineer. Some people like Murray Head were filming and Ian Gillen was busy with Deep Purple so we had to record them when they had a chance. The last song we recorded was "I Don't Know How to Love Him". We recorded it three times with two other girls, and it was a disaster although everybody said it was the best song in the show.

20 Andrew: We had almost finished the recording and we still hadn't found the right Mary Magdelene or a Pilate. I went down to the Pheasantry to see somebody for Pilate and before he came on Yvonne sang and I knew immediately she was it. She's just incredible. Then we found Barry Dennen for Pilate and we had everybody. I mean Pilate like Herod are a bit two dimensional but of course opera is a bit two dimensional that's what makes it so theatrical. Things like "Peter Grimes" and "Tosca" are marvellously theatrical but not exactly what you'd call in-depth portraits.

21 Tim: Finally in June it was finished having by the grace of Brian Brolly and Alan Crowder of MCA cost £14,500 which was the figure deducted from our first royalty cheque.

22 Andrew: Very economical I would say for a work of that length.

23 Tim: Then just as we were putting the finishing touches on the mix the crisis of the cover started. I remember the first one submitted showed Christ languishing in a cell. It was awful. . . Then they had a competition among readers of the NME and that failed to produce anything. We hated all of them. Finally MCA hired a design team and I must say that I like the album although originally the design was a bit complicated structurally which led one reviewer to say that it took longer to get the record out of the packet than it did to play it.

24 Andrew: The American packaging w completely different because they were trying to make it seem very dignified like a traditional recorded opera.

25 Tim: When it came out here we knew in about three minutes that it was going to be a flop because it just didn't get air play.

26 Andrew: Or as one of the reviewers said "Caught between the older generation which thought it was blasphemous and the younger which thought it was boring" it ju sank.

27 Tim: A few months previously an amazing couple from New York called Agnes and John Stoeckert had come over and raved about 'Joseph' which they had seen performed at a seminary on Long Island. Then Barry Kittleson who was our publicist came over and raved about the record. These people gave us some indication of the reaction in America but really nothing compared to what actually happened which at times was really unbelievable.

28 Andrew: MCA had a matching claus for the film and stage rights and we got offers from Harold Fielding, Gordon Mills and Warner Brothers. All the time David an Sefton were particularly keen we should ta one from Robert Stigwood.

29 Tim: We were in New York for the record and David kept getting cables in London from people like David Merrick an Hal Prince saying "I produced 'West Side

of writes a line and then I'll do the music after that, but broadly spea ing I do the music first. FROST: Now what was the first thing y wrote? Was it the number that we did on my show in London a coup of years ago? ANDREW: We did about six numbers, actually. We did

Visit to Jerusalem.

Story' 'My Fair Lady' etc. etc. Please ring me at . . ." All these people made the mistake of getting us to ring them or sending round a minion whereas Robert sent round a Cadillac and we zapped round to his place and we liked him.

30 Andrew: Then Robert had a matching option while other people let theirs drop. He then formed a limited partnership with MCA and finally bought out Superstar Ventures. Of course having made the decision to go with all of this we know we probably lost some of our control—to what extent we will probably never know. But we do know that an awful lot of people made just as much, if not a great deal more money than we have from 'Superstar'.

31 Tim: I suppose that's inevitable where so much money is involved.

32 Andrew: No, the main thing is that we had control over every little aspect of the album and as soon as it started becoming bigger we lost that control.

33 Tim: You know the other morning I was wondering if there was any mail and then I thought "why am I wondering if there is any mail" because I couldn't think of anything in the post that would make me particularly happy. I didn't mean that I was unhappy or anything but I mean after 'Superstar' even if Robert says "I've got something that can make you two million quid and even if he really thinks it could and even if it did I'd think, 'well so what?'

don't know how to love him' and 'Hosanna' and a few things and the overall idea, and the record company who released it decided to select the song 'Superstar', that was the first one to be recorded. FROST: Oh, the first to be recorded, but one of the first....TIM: We conceived it as a

St. John the Baptist's Mission.

whole, I mean as a whole opera, but as we were totally unknown, we wouldn't have got any backing from anybody to record a sort of £20,000 opera, so we had to play....ANDREW: We thought we were never going to get it. TIM: Yes. So they said, look, we'll trust you for a

Baptism of Christ.

OVERTURE

HEAVEN ON THEIR MINDS

UDAS

My mind is clearer now—at last all too well
I can see where we all soon will be
If you strip away the myth from the man
you will see where we all soon will be
Jesus! You've started to believe
The things they say of you
You really do believe
This talk of God is true
And all the good you've done
Will soon get swept away
You've begun to matter more
Than the things you say

Listen Jesus I don't like what I see
All I ask is that you listen to me
And remember—I've been your right hand man all along
You have set them all on fire
They think they've found the new Messiah
And they'll hurt you when they find they're wrong

I remember when this whole thing began
No talk of God then—we called you a man
And believe me—my admiration for you hasn't died
But every word you say today
Gets twisted round some other way
And they'll hurt you if they think you've lied

single if you can choose a two and a half minute or three minute
selection, you know, and we can sort of try the market out with that,
which is in fact what they did with the song 'Superstar'. FROST: What's
the key line in 'Jesus Christ Superstar'? Someone said that you felt that

Temptation of Christ.

Nazareth your famous son should have stayed
   a great unknown
Like his father carving wood—he'd have made good
Tables chairs and oaken chests would have suited Jesus bes*
He'd have caused nobody harm—no-one alarm
Listen Jesus do you care for your race?
Don't you see we must keep in our place?
We are occupied—have you forgotten how put down we are*
I am frightened by the crowd
For we are getting much too loud
And they'll crush us if we go too far
Listen Jesus to the warning I give
Please remember that I want us to live
But it's sad to see our chances weakening with every hour
All your followers are blind
Too much heaven on their minds
It was beautiful but now it's sour
Yes it's all gone sour

WHAT'S THE BUZZ
Bethany, Friday night

APOSTLES

What's the buzz? Tell me what's happening

JESUS
Why should you want to know?
Don't you mind about the future, don't you try
   to think ahead
Save tomorrow for tomorrow, think about today instead

What's the buzz? Tell me what's happening

I could give you facts and figures—I could give you plans
   and forecasts Even tell you where I'm going—

the key line was 'Don't get me wrong, I only want to know'. ANDREW
Oh yes, that's it. TIM: For both of us, yes. FROST: Why....why is th.
the key line 'Don't get me wrong, I only want to know'? TIM: We wan
to emphasize really that Superstar is first and foremost....it's a question

Testimony of the Baptist.

the village VOICE *November 27, 1969*

scenes

CHRIST AND ROCK 'n' roll have not had a good relationship. Remember that "we are more popular than Jesus" John Lennon craziness a couple of years ago, and the censorship of the "Christ you know it ain't easy" line in a recent Beatles single.

Keeping all that in mind, I can imagine what the reaction is going to be to "Superstar," a new British single about to be released in this country by Decca. Just one song from a rock opera called "Jesus Christ," "Superstar" has been for sale in London a few weeks but its lyrics are already stirring things up. Bible belt radio stations over hear are going to have 50,000-watt heart attacks over such lines as: "Did you mean to die like that? was that a mistake or/Did you know your messy death would be a record-breaker? /Don't you get me wrong /I only want to know /Jesus Christ Jesus Christ Who are you? What have you sacrificed? /Jesus Christ Superstar Do you think you're what they say you are?" (Copyright 1969 by Leeds Music Ltd., London, England. Used by permission, all rights reserved.)

The complete opera will be performed in venerable St. Paul's Cathedral early next year and then released as an album. The dean of St. Paul's, who fully supports the pop opera, defended the lyrics as a powerful and urgent inquiry. "There are some people who may be shocked by this record," he explained. "I ask them to listen to it and think again. It is a desperate cry . . . The record probes some answers and makes some comparisons. The onus is on the listener to come up with his replies. If he is a Christian, let him answer for Christ. The singer says, 'Don't get me wrong. I only want to know.' He is entitled to some response."

And he will undoubtedly get one. Even if the performers involved in the opera, like singer Murray Head, Joe Cocker's Grease Band, and Juicy Lucy, don't make it a hit album, somewhere deep in God-fearing country they already may be preparing to nail Decca to the cross.

—Howard Smith

"He'd be ideal for the part." said the producers of a pop musical about Christ called "Superstar." "After all, from pictures of Christ he looked like a well-turned-out Lennon." John Lennon, that is, Sure, he'd consider playing Jesus, the Beatle was reported to have said, "but if I do it, I would want Yoko Ono to play Mary Magdalene." The Dean of St. Paul's Cathedral in London, where they hope to stage "Superstar," explained hastily that he had "nothing to do with the casting." By then, the producers were getting a little nervous too, and the offer was withdrawn.

Time

s not a statement. We weren't trying to say anything to anybody in e sense of this is how it was, this is how all young people today think, s is what....you know, we are spokesmen for our generation. This is mpletely untrue. Really 'Superstar' to us, and this may sound strange,

Early Disciples.

New Label -- New Artist -- New Smash

Shortly you will be receiving a keg of dynamite in the form & shape of a record.

Title: "Superstar"
Artist: Silver Metre - Recorded in England
Label: National General
Prediction: #1

But.....

...there is another version of this same song already out on the market...on Decca Records...by Murray Head (whoever he is!).

We Suggest...

1st - Service Ours

2nd - Have your stations play them back to back...and we will get the airplay!!!
We have a better record.

There will be CASH offered on Silver Metre. Start early 'cause we back you 100%.

Let's teach that sleeping giant just how POWERFUL our promo forces really are!!!

On National General, of course!!!

DECCA RECORDS
DIVISION
NEW YORK
N.Y.

INTER·OFFICE COMMUNICATION

RECD. JAN 27 1970
Date: January 26, 1970

Copies:

To: Decca Field Force
From: Harold Komisar
Subject: "Superstar"

As you probably are all aware of by now, we have a competitive record out on "Superstar". I said competitive, but let me water it down by saying that our version - the original version of "Superstar" - is by far the best. I've attached a letter sent out by the Buddah office and sent to their field force hyping their version and kind of putting down the Decca sales and promotion force... I want you to read the attached carefully and let your blood boil because, I'll tell you in front, I'm hopping mad! If Buddah wants to refer to us as a "sleeping giant", we'll let everyone know that the "sleeping giant" is wide awake and ready for battle!

Whatever you've done in the past to obtain air play and exposure for our "Superstar", I want you to triple your efforts now. That means each and every salesman and promotion man - whether you're independent or part of the branch sales force - I want this record carried in your car and played on every call that you make. I won't tolerate any account calling me and saying that they haven't "Superstar" in stock. At our Decca meeting we talked about "BASICS". This is where the basics really come in. This is where you can show little Buddah that the giant is not only awake, but running and running fast.

GENTLEMEN, I HAVE NO INTENTION OF LOSING THIS RECORD TO ANY COMPANY. YOU MUST RUN AND RUN HARD. WE MUST HAVE YOUR FULL AND UTMOST COOPERATION. BE YOU INDEPENDENT OR BRANCH OPERATION. I EMPHASIZE THAT. I WANT THIS RECORD BROUGHT HOME!

Regards,
[signature]

HK:as

P.S. Remember - we not only have the original single but the original cast LP "Superstar" to be released shortly.

---

but it's just what we think is a good record and that's all we rea
wanted it to be: a good, serious, but entertaining record and all this s
of huge paraphanelia, you know, which has now got as far as Broadw
....obviously we are flattered and delighted that our work has be

First Miracle at Cana.

GREAT BRITAIN

INTER-OFFICE COMMUNICATION

Date	10 March 1970	Copies to	Earle Adams	At	LIC
From	Brian Brolly		Jack Loetz		New York
To	Dick Broderick		Cyril Simons		London
	New York		Henry Thomas		London
Subject	JESUS CHRIST				

The Jesus Christ Rock Opera has now been written. It is excellent and will be a two-record set.

We are currently trying to arrange the casting of the singers for the major voices as well as for the rhythm and rock groups. They hopefully expect to have these arrangements completed in the next two weeks.

We plan to record during March and April and would not have a finished tape until May. The earliest possible release date, therefore, looks like being June. It may make a great deal of sense to consider the release of the album in America with ourselves following in September.

We hopefully will record at the beginning of our recording sessions two songs that will lend themselves to exploitation as singles and based entirely on their merit and strength we would propose the release of a further single as we would not have an immediate follow-up of an album to the success of the Superstar single.

We are developing our ideas in respect of the artwork in order that we can at least have this ready by the time recording and mixing are completed.

During the next two weeks we will endeavour to conclude contractual arrangements with artists and resolve any problems with regard to our rights in the recording and copyright of the music.

BTB:vf

---

1 CHARLES STREET.
MAYFAIR. LONDON. W.1.
01-499 888

Jack Loetz Esq
Decca Records
445 Park Avenue
NEW YORK
NY 10023
U.S.A.

22 May 1970

Dear Jack:

Thank you very much for all the help and hospitality you gave to us during our recent visit to the Decca offices. We were delighted and surprised at the great interest everybody showed in our work and we are currently working at top speed to give you more product in the form of the album. Murray's single will be with you next week as soon as we have mixed the track. We have added the orchestra already.

We are writing directly to Bill Levy about the cover crisis and we have also written to Barry Kittleson whom we met in New York and whom we shall be in close direct touch with concerning all publicity and press.

We look forward to seeing you again shortly either in England or in America and hope that you will understand that we are going flat out and how to finish the JESUS CHRIST/SUPERSTAR album - a mammoth project, but we hope a successful one.

With best wishes

Yours sincerely,

ANDREW LLOYD WEBBER   TIM RICE

---

epted, but it has got very out of control inasmuch as people now t of regard Superstar almost as something on a par with the formation as a watershed in religious history, which is ludicrous, I an, I think....it's a very good record but....FROST: Take the

First Cleansing of the Temple.

"He who has ears t

Broadway production, which is what, 700....you mentioned 20,0
pounds to do a record, but the Broadway budget was whatever it w
700,000 dollars or whatever. Now did you have in mind when y
originally wrote the song 'Superstar', did you have in mind someth

Interview with Nicodemus.

"There's nothing in
there for Vera Lynn
or Ruby Murray"

Cyril Simons
Leeds Music
Publishing (UK)

the way it turned out on Broadway? ANDREW: Well I think that
ly, I mean, we wrote the thing also because we were very fascinated
the figure of Christ as a man as I think, you know, virtually
ybody must be who is at all influenced, you know, by anything in

Visit to Samaria.

JESUS CHRIST SUPERSTAR

(A Rock Opera)/Overture - Heaven On Their Minds - What's The Buzz/Strange Thing Mystifying - Everything's Alright - This Jesus Must Die - Hosanna - Simon Zealotes/Poor Jerusalem - Pilate's Dream - The Temple - Everything's Alright - I Don't Know How To Love Him - Damned For All Time/Blood Money - The Last Supper - Gethsemane (I Only Want To Say) - The Arrest - Peter's Denial - Pilate And Christ - King Herod's Song (Try It And See) - Juda's Death - Trial Before Pilate (Including The 39 Lashes) - Superstar - Crucifixion - John Nineteen Forty-One. (DL 79178-79) Recorded In England. Available Only In U.S.A. And Canada.
(S)
DXSA 7206
6-6000
C73-6000

SCOTT CHRISTOPHER MORE SWITCHED ON BACHARACH

Christopher Scott. Raindrops Keep Fallin' On My Head - Wishin' And Hopin' - (There's) Always Something There To Remind Me - (They Long To Be) Close To You - Everybody's Out Of Town - Paper Mache - A Message To Michael - I'll Never Fall In Love Again - Reach Out For Me - Promises, Promises - Trains And Boats And Planes.
(S)
DL 75243
6-5243
C73-5243

our Western Society at all. He is an incredibly interesting figure becau one is brought up with Him and we really wanted to try and write som thing, as I think we said to you ages ago in London when the Dean St. Paul's was involved with it in the initial stages, which was about H

Healing of the Nobleman's Son at Capernaum.

GREAT BRITAIN
RECD. AUG 31 1970 INTER-OFFICE COMMUNICATION

Date	27 August 1970	Copies to	Mike Maitland	At	UC
From	Brian Brolly		Dick Broderick		New York
To	Jack Loetz		Tony Martell		New York
At	New York				
Subject	JESUS CHRIST — SUPERSTAR				
	ROCK OPERA				

We have cut our master lacquers and test pressings in the
form of white label copies and these will shortly be sent
to you. We have already shipped tapes to those countries
who will be immediately manufacturing the record. We
will be able to send sleeve proofs, outside and inside,
and the libretto at the end of August.

This is a truly phenomenal work. I know how excited
you have been in anticipation. I have personally spent
much of myself and the Company's money in the completion
of this Opera. I have no doubts at all of its
outstanding aesthetic values and absolutely no doubt
that creative and agressive selling and promotion will
make this set one of the biggest selling albums in our
history.

I look forward to your own personal reaction and
commitment to help bring this home.

Kind regards,

BTB:bf

man and we really wanted something that was perhaps a kind of
racter....a study of the characters. I think the record is to an extent
udy of the characters and I think this is probably more how we see
FROST: The record is more the way you see it than the stage show?

Miracle at the Pool of Bethesda.

Dick Broderick Esq
MCA Records
445 Park Avenue
New York City
NY 10023
U.S.A.

3 September 1970

Dear Dick:

Everybody in our offices has just tottered back from a wide variety of holiday
and we are all set to go with the promotion campaign for JESUS CHRIST/
SUPERSTAR in a big way. All is going well with the cover, booklet and the
actual cuts themselves, about which I am sure you are fully posted by MCA-U

Naturally we are keen to know what is cooking in the US promotion campaig
and as we wish to co-ordinate our efforts with yours I thought it might be a g
idea to set down a few basic outlines of what we are planning to do and what
would like to do. I understand David Land may also have written to your off
but at the risk of duplicating information, here are the points we are currentl
concerned about.

1. We would be grateful to receive US test pressings of the album before the
records are pressed just in case there is any discrepancy between the tracks or
pressings and the information in the booklet—we have no worries about the
technical quality of the cuts (naturally!) but we made several mistakes oursel
with the gaps between the tracks before we got it right in England.

2. We plan to send Don Norman over to New York on or about September 2
a few days in order that he may liaise with you and your promotion and pub
men to prepare interviews, press, radio and TV or whatever else could help th
album, for Andrew and myself when we come over in October for the record
actual release. Don will be able to liaise with Greg Hirsch, Barry Kittleson an
anybody who could help in this matter. Don is keen to deal with all sectors o
promotion from the underground to Time Magazine, and he would also like t
the album to any religious leaders who would provide good quotes and opinic
for use in the campaign. Don has in fact just returned to Finland on a similar
mission which proved a very successful trip—in particular a session in a huge
beautiful modern church before a panel of religious leaders where the whole
was played attracted a large amount of publicity and press reaction.

3. Don will bring over tapes, pressings, photographs, handouts etc., including
short tapes of some of the individual songs from the opera which could be of
for radio play. He will also be able to bring quotes from us, cover mock-ups i

**TIM: Well, we always wanted to see it as either a stage show or a
or both and we see the Broadway production as Tom O'Horg
interpretation of it, which works very well for Broadway. Perha
isn't how we would see it, but everybody sees this story, which is a**

Preaching in the Synagogue at Nazareth.

STLES
When do we ride into Jerusalem?

US
Why should you want to know?
Why are you obsessed with fighting times and fates
  you can't defy?
you knew the path we're riding you'd understand it
  less than I

STLES
What's the buzz? Tell me what's happening

RY MAGDALENE
Let me try to cool down your face a bit

US
That feels nice, so nice…
Mary that is good—
While you prattle through your supper—where and when
  and who and how
he alone has tried to give me what I need
  right here and now

STLES
What's the buzz? Tell me what's happening?

STRANGE THING MYSTIFYING

AS

It seems to me a strange thing, mystifying
That a man like you can waste his time
on women of her kind
es I can understand that she amuses
ut to let her stroke you, kiss your hair, is hardly in your line

sonal story for everybody, in thousands and thousands of different
s and we really hope that the work will be done in different places
nd the world in endlessly different versions. ANDREW: Yes, I am
to say that they are....that a lot of people are doing it in other

Second Call of Four Apostles.

But she doesn't fit in well with what you teach and say
It doesn't help us if you're inconsistent
They only need a small excuse to put us all away

JESUS
Who are you to criticise her? Who are you to despise her?
Leave her, leave her, let her be now
Leave her, leave her, she's with me now
If your slate is clean—then you can throw stones
If your slate is not then leave her alone
I'm amazed that men like you can be
    so shallow thick and slow
There is not a man among you who knows
    or cares if I come or go

ALL (save JUDAS)
No you're wrong! You're very wrong!
    How can you say that?

JESUS
Not one—not one of you!

EVERYTHING'S ALRIGHT

MARY MAGDALENE
Try not to get worried, try not to turn on to
Problems that upset you oh don't you know
Everything's alright yes everything's fine
And we want you to sleep well tonight
Let the world turn without you tonight
If we try we'll get by so forget all about us tonight

APOSTLES' WOMEN
Everything's alright yes everything's alright yes

countries in quite a different way, only for us as authors, it's
interesting to kind of go and see, I mean we were kind of outsiders
sense on this particular production, we sort of arrived and sort of
it, as it were, and you know, I think there are going to be things we

Miracles in and around Capernaum.

*dy and a host of wondrous things. If you have any particular requests in this
e, please inform us.*

*Will you be releasing a single from the album to tie in with the album release?
so which? If so, will you want any publicity material, such as film clips? Will
u want any film clips anyway even if you are not releasing a single? Will the
pearance of any of the cast in New York be of any help to you? We would have
know about film clips and about anything connected with the cast as soon as
ssible as they all have tight schedules in connection with their own work.*

*Did anything/will anything happen to the radio interview with Fred Robbins?
n we hear it before it escapes or even improve on it for you?*

*Should Don do anything about Canada or is this done through your offices?
re Canada putting it out?)*

*We then plan to come over in mid-October for a trip that would be largely
nned out well before we got there. Provided the seeds of interest are sown well
all concerned in good time, I am sure our appearance would be of colossal value
the promotion campaign. If we can be of any use in chatting to dealers,
resentatives of MCA on the road or in any sphere whatsoever, we are of course
lighted to do so. We look forward anyway to meeting you in London around
ptember 10 when we can all discuss these and any other points.*

*action to the album has been universally excellent this end—we hope the same
true in America.*

th all best wishes.

n Rice   c.c. Jack Loetz Esq

"hat's what I respected about Tim and Andrew — they knew what would sell —
d in Heaven — they knew."

Barry Kittleson
Press Agent

ster Grace
. Peter's Church

ear Sister Grace:

It was a pleasure for Mr. Milt Gabler and myself to meet with
ou and Pastor Peterson Monday afternoon. As you will see from the
closed we are preparing a rather important and significant release

don't like in lots of productions. FROST: What did you like and
like in this production? ANDREW: Well, it's a big question. I think,
ve all slightly Breugelish overtones that he has brought into the first
I personally would just like to see something that was a little bit

Call of Levi.

of the "Jesus Christ Superstar," Rock Opera album. We feel that it will be a meaningful religious experience in the music idiom that ha something to say for everyone of today.

It is our intention to present the album in tape concert perfor mance before members of the daily wire services the weekly period als such as Time, Life, Look, etc., TV, radio, Madison Avenue, and religious periodicals in a setting that would lend proper listening atmosphere for the reviewers. We would like to invite about 250 people and feel that your chapel would be perfect for our needs. Again, let me point out that we will not instigate any salesmanship or do anything crassly commercial.

We would like the afternoon of Tuesday, October 27, 3:00 to 5:00 PM. As Paster Peterson pointed out, this would be during Reformation Week and would add considerable significance.

Decca Records would be pleased to make a donation of $ 400 for the two hour program.

A courteous and efficient recording staff would set up a porta tape sound system, and the event would be handled with impeccab taste. The writers and producers will be coming in from England an will add dignity to the occasion.

Please let me hear from you at your earliest convenience.

Best Regards,

Tom Morgan
Director Artist & Repertoire

"I wanted it to be extremely dignified — I didn't want to give them any cause say 'how could they do that? It's bad enough to use the name Jesus Christ but this!' So I said if it's an opera let's treat it like an opera"

Bill Le
Director of Creative Servi

more concerned with the characterization and the characters becau think that the piece has weaknesses, we agree that, because it was first attempt really, apart from that Joseph thing we did. I mea was our first shot at it and we wrote it two years ago and we char

Blessed are the poor in spirit: for theirs is the kingdom of heaven.

TIME

Jesus Christ Superstar
Rocks Broadway

AUSTRIA . . . . S 13
BELGIUM . . . . F 25
CZECHOSLOVAKIA Kcs 7.25
DENMARK . . . . . . Kr 4.00
FINLAND . . . . . . Fmk 2.00

FRANCE . . . . 2.80 FF
GERMANY . . . . . DM 2.00
GIBRALTAR 20np
GREECE . . . . Dr 15
ICELAND . Kr 40 (incl. tax)

IRELAND . 20np (incl. tax)
ISRAEL . . . . IL 2.00
ITALY . . . . Lit 300
LUXEMBOURG . . . B.Fr 25
NETHERLANDS . . Fl 2.00

NORWAY . . . . Kr 3.50
POLAND . . . . Zl 20
PORTUGAL . . . . . . Esc 15
SPAIN . . . . Ptas 35

SWEDEN . Kr 3.20 (incl.
SWITZERLAND . . . .
YUGOSLAVIA . . . .
UNITED KINGDOM
U.S. ARMED FORC

ROLLING STONE

NEW YORK—*Jesus Christ—Superstar,* the so-called "serious rock opera" about the seven last days of Christ with lyrics by Tim Rice and music by Andrew Lloyd Webber, was unveiled at St. Peter's Lutheran Church October 27th in front of a congregation including the usual press, radio, and promotion entourage, "clergymen of all denominations," and other friends of musical uplift.

The presentation preceded the release of the two-record album "package" which Decca is describing as "one of the most monumental rock recording projects ever undertaken." It featured Messrs. Rice and Webber standing in alternate turns at a lectern, narrating and illuminating the opera's dramatic progression as the music rose (wafter? wailed?) through the stained-glass lit spaces. And just before the altar, reverently placed, was a translucent screen on which slides designed by Bill Levy flashed all the portentous lyrics against a background of *groovy* mediaeval and renaissance paintings—angles from the Sistine Chapel, gothic church facades, and angels making a joyful noise.

Messrs. Rice and Webber are talented and clever young Englishmen who command smooth lyrical and dramatic gifts. They originally had looked around for a "subject" for an opera and having thought of doing something on the Cuban Missile Crisis (!), they decided finally to take hold of the greatest story ever told ("That's a heavy one, too," a promoter might have said.) According to Webber: "We're trying to tell a fascinating story and get over the political aspects of the time and re-evaluate the story."

The opera is well-made. Through-composed and strophic elements cohere, jangly and snappy rhythmic juxtapositions create a sense of flow

 our mind about a lot of it, but I think that if it's made intimate, in a way that might, that might, for me work better. But that might not work in a theatre. TIM: I think it has problems occasionally when our department's weak, now and then it doesn't work and often the fault is

Blessed are they that mourn: for they shall be comforted.

and continuity. There's an overture full of motifs in the best *bel canto* and Broadway manner and an instrumental Crucifixion passage of sustained quarter-tone pitches a la Ligeti and Lennie Tristano-type piano figurations overlapping.

The opera's derivative quality is exposed in innumerable ways. But primarily the tone the music and words create is one of forced hipness and sentimentality, that of an egregiously over-sweet rock-coated Broadway musical. There are the dramatic declamatory descending modulations when Jesus sings of understanding what power really is about, a steal from *Tommy's* "How can he be saved/From the eternal grave."

When Jesus rails at the polluters of the temple, his wailing ways sound more like Jimi Hendrix calling on his foxy lady than someone expressing a fine sense of moral outrage. And this is followed by a wispy, reflective passage that would have been more appropriate as a moment of the adolescent-dumb gloom Johnny Mathis might have felt after losing his latest passion.

Then there are the lyrics: "What's the buzz?" ask the apostles; "Tell me what's happening?" And Mary Magdalene: "I'm the one who's always been/So calm, so cool, no lover's fool," she sings, a sweet half-groupie, half-teenaged ballad for Jesus, the man she doesn't know how to love. And all the while Italian night club imitation rock music adjoining strings and horns create an embarrassing but melodious scene.

It's not so much that the opera sounds more like Francoise Hardy ye-ye than the Who (which is to say that the opera doesn't rock all that much), but that it does nothing to enrich, expand, uncover, or commit itself to any personal vision, in the sense that Pasolini and Rossellini have transformed the Gospels in their films. Frankie Lymon and the Teenagers or Ray Davies would have had more to say or see about Jesus.

Jesus Christ—Superstar includes an all-star cast: Deep Purple's Ian Gillan sings the role of Jesus, Mike d'Abo of Manfred Mann plays Herod, and Murray Head, who sang the "Superstar" hit from the opera—half a million copes sold as a single—is Judas. The recording features a six piece rock band consisting of former members of Joe Cocker's Greaseband and Juicy Lucy, an 85-piece symphony orchestra, and three choirs. Decca is backing the opera with a massive advertising and promotional campaign.

Ministers and priests have been mobilized: "I was deeply moved," Father Kenneth Jadoff has said. Reverend Dr. Ernest R. Palen states: "To me, now over 40 years in the ministry, it was an amazing revelation of the deeper spiritual and meaningful subjects to which rock music can really be turned."

One can imagine how church

us because we sort of wrote it as a record initially, which it works yo know....ANDREW: We wrote for, you know, further production, mean this is the idea, but....FROST: But it's amazing, I mean a fantasti tribute to hear them talk of this as your first attempt when....what

Blessed are the meek: for they shall inherit the earth.

officials will see in *Jesus Christ–Superstar* a chance to revitalize young parishioners' waning faith and turn the tides of all nefarious Post-Christian though with just a listen. And beyond this, movie and stage offers are coming in by the score. Things have reached such a pitch that Webber and Rice have been offered money *not* to sign anything.

"We're interested in getting the opera put on in a way that's artistically right," Andrew Webber says. "We had in mind a claustrophobic setting—Jerusalem as a little town." Both he and Rice insist on retaining control over any stage productions.

Neither Rice nor Webber is a professed true believer. "We're not trying to pull people's beliefs away," Webber says, "but I personally don't think that Jesus is God. We tried to put over what we think might have happened. Pilate tries to keep it cooler for the bosses in Rome, for instance. And I think that Christ as a liberal reformer was a huge success. Slowly the thing got out of control. People began to worship Christ and not the cause. And Judas was shit scared, for political reasons.

"One of the things that started me thinking about Judas was the line in Dylan's song: 'I can't think for you, you'll have to decide/Did Judas Iscariot have God on his side.' The answer in my case is: no. Judas was an intelligent man. What he says is well thought-out. He was the treasurer, and it must have been annoying for him to see all the funds go on Nivea cream. He was concerned that everything Christianity stood for would be wiped out if Christ got too big. Judas is saying: Get back to where you once belonged.

"Judas was a kind of Everyman. If Christ has come along some other time, the media would have made him known to be just a man. When you saw Bobby Kennedy or Martin Luther King you could de-deify them."

"Rock can communicate instantly," Tim Rice adds. "When I was younger I was an admirer of both Prokofiev's *Love of the Three Oranges* and Bill Haley. Alban Berg and Stockhausen appeal to the esoteric few. But when Pink Floyd did *Saucerful of Secrets,* they translated Stockhausen, say, for a greater audience.

"Melody in rock is unoriginal, for the most part. Intervallically it's not very interesting. I've used certain themes in the opera. There's a questioning kind of theme riff at the beginning representing the hostile elements which oppose Jesus. And there's an emotive theme for Christ in Gethsemene.

"One is hoping one's music will improve. I've been commissioned to write a concerto for rock guitar and the London Symphony Orchestra. And I think it would be great if Jimmy Page would be interested in performing it."

Further church presentations of the opera will shortly occur at the West Hollywood Presbyterian Church

he prediction....how much is the show going to gross by the time it as finished? TIM: Well, I mean....FROST: Well, what do people tell s? TIM: I don't know, I mean....ANDREW: We had some amazing igures all the time. FROST: What ones do you hear? ANDREW: I

Blessed are they that hunger and thirst after righteousness: for they shall be filled.

in Los Angeles and at churches in Toronto, Chicago, Atlanta, and Dallas. And, as Decca points out, copies of the album are being sent to religious leaders throughout the country.

In spite of the opera's occasional lyrical felicities and the professionalism with which it is put together, you might well feel that there's more about the limits of suffering and hopes for redemption in Dylan's "Just Like Tom Thumb's Blues", for example, with its Eastertime setting in Juarez and its visiting saints and angels from the coast. You might listen to *Jesus Christ–Superstar* on the radio, hear it in church, and then get to your local record store and pick up Karl Richter's version of Bach's *St. Matthew Passion*, a copy of Dylan's Mighty Quinn, or a Swan Silvertones album instead.

"At first I admit I wasn't in favour of it. I thought, you know, Christ and the Royal Family, that sort of thing was akin to . . . I didn't want to offend anybody. So I suggested that we sent copies to the Dean of St. Paul's, the Dean of Westminster and the Archbishop of Canterbury to make sure there was no offence."

David Land

"There are some people who may be shocked by this record. I ask them to listen to it and think again. It is a desperate cry. Who are you Jesus Christ? is the urgent inquiry, and a very proper one at that. The record probes some of the answers and makes some comparisons The onus is on the listener to come up with his replies. If he is a Christian let him answer for Christ. The singer says, 'Don't get me wrong. I only want to know.' He is entitled to some response."

The Very Reverend Martin Sullivan
Dean of St. Paul.

RR OCTOBER 10, 1970

The question is – will 'Superstar' collect super sales?

don't know, I think if the film....TIM: I honestly don't know, but mean it is booked up you know. ANDREW: I think we can truthful say, I don't think we really care. I can truthfully say that I real think we tried to write something that we never dreamt, in our wilde

Controversy with regard to Work on the Sabbath.

It's just about 225 years since Johann Sebastian Bach's "St. Matthew Passion" was first produced in Thomaskirche. It was a revolutionary work, scored for three choruses, two orchestras, two organs and soloists. But the key to the vastness of the three hour drama was Bach's profound conception of the Christ. Like most revolutionary works, it was received with bewilderment. 'God help us," wrote one critic, " 'tis surely an opera-comedy."

We were reminded of this the other night upon hearing the new rock opera written by Andrew Lloyd Webber and Tim Rice based on the seven last days of Christ, previewed here at the West Hollywood Presbyterian Church. The new Decca 2 pocket LP set is titled "Jesus Christ Superstar" and features members (past and present) of such groups as Deep Purple, Joe Cocker's Grease Band, Lord Sutch, Aynsley Dunbar Retaliation, Merseybeats, Gracious, Nucleus, an 85 piece symphony orchestra and the strings of the city of London. The work is a proteen exhibition of secular, ecclesiastical, folk, rock, blues, jazz, ragtime, fugues, pop and symphonic sounds. It is, at once, pretentious, compelling, redundant, thunderous and historic. In months, and perhaps years, to come it will be alternately damned and praised. Like "Hair" or the modern dress version of "Julius Caesar" it will shock and even disgust. It will also undoubtedly be an enormous commercial success. Some are already claiming that it is the most monumental rock release since "Rubber Soul" or "Sgt. Pepper." "Arresting," is one of the early quotes we've received. It comes from the Dean of St. Paul's Church in England. And from the Reverend Dr. Ernest R. Palen, Minister of the Middle Collegiate Church in Manhattan, "It is an amazing revelation of the deeper spiritual and meaningful subjects to which rock music can really be turned."

A copywriter for Decca contents, "It is safe to assume that this work will capture the imagination of almost every American. In fact, Jesus Christ/Superstar is well on its way to bridging the musical and scriptual generation gap. If ever anything was written for all ages, it is Jesus Christ/Superstar."

Leeds Music Ltd., publishers of most of the score, already reports single versions of some of the songs: Mary Magdalene's solos, "Everything's Alright" and "I Don't Know How to Love Him." Both are hummable top forty material. The title tune, released last year, has already sold half a million singles world wide.

The set cost a reported $65,000 to produce. It was cut at the Olympic Sound Studios, Barnes, Advision Studios, Island Studios and Spot Production Studios in England on 16 track tape. It will retail at $11.98 (discount stores will probably be selling it at $8.99). Decca has pressed 100,000 sets and is presently shipping to distribs. Several thousand of the English pressings have already found their way into record shops throughout the country.

The current issue of Time Magazine devotes a full page rave to the package, we're told. But that's only the beginning. You'll undoubtedly be reading and hearing and talking about this opera into '71 and beyond. And that because, despite it's deficiencies, it is one of the very important albums of the decade. Again, reminding us of verse 25 from the Gospel According to John (21) "And there are also so many other things which Jesus did, the which, if they should be written every one, I suppose that even the world itself could not contain the books that should be written. Amen." Jesus Christ/Superstar is another, not final, chapter. Still it's a brave, substantial and majestic experience.

imagination, would do this. We'd never been to America in our lives til last year. I mean when we sort of arrived with our sort of record and everything, we were absolutely amazed that there was this interest in it. FROST: Because it was a smash here and not in England. TIM: It

Healing on the Sabbath.

DEREK JEWELL

Caught in the crossfire between an older generation, who may regard it as distasteful or even sacrilegious, and a younger who could be deterred or scornfu because of its religious associations, life is perhaps going to be hard for Jesus Christ, Superstar, which is sad.

This is the title of a remarkable "rock opera" (a misleading label) issued last week as a double album by MCA (£3. 19s 10d) and composed by two artist in their twenties, Tim Rice (lyricist) and Andrew Lloyd Webber (composer), who two years ago cut their teeth on this kind of epic by producing "Joseph an the Amazing Technicolour Dreamcoat", an entertaining but altogether lighter piece which was first performed by a pop group and the choir and orchestra of Colet Court, the St. Paul's junior school.

"Superstar" lasts almost one and a half hours. It is an imaginative re-creat founded on the Biblical record, of the immediate events leading to the Crucifix It uses many rock techniques, as well as those of twentieth-century formal com position, and as an artistic exercise in musical drama is every bit as valid as (an to me, often more moving than) Handel's "Messiah" which, similarly, clothed the Christian story in the language, melodic and verbal, of its day.

Rice has gone further than Handel, though. He has consciously compoun ed into the powerful narrative some of the attitudes of our day. This is most clearly seen in the treatment of Judas.

Without in any way injuring the idea and character of Christ as Son of God which the Bible portrays, Judas is presented far more sympathetically—a realist who had supported Jesus as a liberal reformer, healing and giving to the poor, but who is frightened once his leader begins to act as God, appearing to head up a rebellion against Rome, which Judas believes will cause the occupyin power to smash their movement.

Listen Jesus to the warning I give,
Please remember that I want us to live.

Judas protests at the annointing of Jesus by Mary Magdalene—because th expensive ointment could have bought food for the starving poor. His betrayal of Christ is a matter of principle, not of personal gain. At the end, in tortured mental conflict, he is screaming
I don't believe he knows I acted for our good,

was a hit almost before we got off the plane, I mean, you know, it v released in London about two weeks before New York and in Lon it sort of came out with a fair bit of publicity and quite good revi and then absolutely nothing and we thought, back to the drawing boa

Call of the Apostles.

Sleep and I shall soothe you, calm you and anoint you
Myrrh for your hot forehead oh then you'll feel
Everything's alright yes everything's fine
And it's cool and the ointment's sweet
For the fire in your head and feet
Close your eyes close your eyes
And relax think of nothing tonight

APOSTLES' WOMEN
Everything's alright yes everything's alright yes

JUDAS
Woman your fine ointment—brand new and expensive
Could have been saved for the poor
Why has it been wasted? We could have raised maybe
Three hundred silver pieces or more
People who are hungry, people who are starving
Matter more than your feet and hair

MARY MAGDALENE
Try not to get worried, try not turn on to
Problems that upset you oh don't you know
Everything's alright yes everything's fine
And we want you to sleep well tonight
Let the world turn without you tonight
If we try we'll get by so forget all about us tonight

APOSTLES' WOMEN
Everything's alright yes everything's alright yes

JESUS
Surely you're not saying we have the resources
To save the poor from their lot?
There will be poor always, pathetically struggling—
Look at the good things you've got!

os, but we still had this trip to America to do and we thought the
e thing will happen there and at least we had one free trip to New
k and as soon as we got there, and there was this air of excitement
'Well, boys, WABC are playing it' and this and that and the other,

The Sermon on the Mount.

Think! while you still have me
Move! while you still see me
You'll be lost and you'll be so sorry when I'm gone

MARY MAGDALENE
Sleep and I shall soothe you, calm you and anoint you
Myrrh for your hot forehead oh then you'll feel
Everything's alright yes everything's fine
And it's cool and the ointment's sweet
For the fire in your head and feet
Close your eyes close your eyes
And relax think of nothing tonight
Close your eyes close your eyes and relax

ALL
Everything's alright yes everything's alright yes

THIS JESUS MUST DIE
Jerusalem, Sunday

PRIEST 1
Good Caiaphas the council waits for you
The Pharisees and priests are here for you

CAIAPHAS
Ah gentlemen—you know why we are here
We've not much time and quite a problem here

MOB outside
Hosanna! Superstar!

ANNAS
Listen to that howling mob of blockheads in the street!
A trick or two with lepers and the whole town's on its feet

ALL
He is dangerous

and it was on the charts in about two days flat and it was so comple
unexpected because it had already flopped in two weeks in Londo
mean discs can flop that quickly, if you don't make it in ten day
something, I mean, you've had it. FROST: Right, that's fascinating, i

Blessed are the merciful: for they shall obtain mercy.

I'd save him all this suffering if I could.

Excoriating as is the stark and wonderfully written scene of the Crucifixion, most anguished section of the whole work is Judas' suicide and the character ven a superb reading by Murray Head (who played in "Hair"). Other names stellar, including Ian Gillan (of Deep Purple) as Christ, Mike d'Abo as Herod, ry Dennen (the MC in the London production of "Cabaret") as Pilate, and a new female voice, Yvonne Elliman, as Mary Magdalene. There are also three irs, more than 30 top jazz and rock musicians (Chris Spedding, Keith istie, Kenny Wheeler among them), a large string orchestra and a Moog thesizer.

Despite passages where concepts defeat both words and music, this is a k on a heroic scale, masterfully conceived, honestly done, and overflowing h splendid music and apt language.

the difference in the two countries. We've got to take a break e and in a moment we're coming back and have got some songs n Jesus Christ Superstar starting with the song from Mary Magdalene in fact we'll talk about that when we come back in a minute after

Blessed are the pure in heart: for they shall see God.

Los Angeles Free Press
Record reviews by Chris VanNess

JESUS CHRIST SUPERSTAR (A rock opera by Andrew Lloyd Webber and Ti
Rice. Produced by Andrew Lloyd Webber and Tim Rice. Decca DXSA-7206.

I never thought that I would find a record important enough to justify takin
up an entire column with just one review, but here I am doing just that. JESUS
CHRIST SUPERSTAR has to be the greatest pop recording produced since the
first African ever pounded a drum.

Now, right away you're probably suspicious of my sanity or judgement (or
both), but I ask only that you listen to the record before pronouncing any ver-
dicts about the state of my mental health. For years people have been trying to
synthesize pop music into a concrete, extended form of expression without rel
ing on established forms. Until JESUS CHRIST SUPERSTAR, nobody had
succeeded.

Granted, TOMMY was a brilliant work, but in actuality it was nothing more
than a suite of songs. While it was labelled a "rock opera". it did not even come
close to being an opera by definition. There have been other attempts at synthe
sis (some of the most recent including the Nice's "Five Bridges" and Pink Floyc
"Atom Heart Mother"); but these too, have remained little more than curiosit

JESUS CHRIST SUPERSTAR is also a "rock opera", but the definition fits;
the only quarrel you might have is with the "rock" part. While rock music as w
know it is used extensively throughout the piece, we are forced to accept Andr
Webber's broad definition of rock in order to accept the label. There is also
electronic music, inspired choral work, classical references and a song and danc
routine that Eddy Foy would have been delighted to use on any vaudeville stag
It is a synthesis of music that goes as far back as Bach and yet is as recent as th
Rolling Stones.

While the opera has never been produced on the stage (the composers consic
it "probably the most expensive demonstration record ever made", since produ
tion is their ultimate goal), it is ready for production in substantially the same
form in which it was recorded.

One of the things that thrills me most about the opera is the basic concept o
treating Christ and those around him on a purely humanistic level. Although th
story is a religious one, the opera is almost antireligious in its treatment. JESUS
CHRIST SUPERSTAR is an historical and humanistic interpretation of the last
seven days of Christ.

Tim Rice, who wrote the libretto, told me that the only sources he used wer
the gospels plus a book by Bishop Fulton Sheen for the historical perspective—

the break because what about the controversy there has been ab
whether you are suggesting that there was a sexual relationship betw
....TIM: I would like to answer this one because....FROST: Je
Christ and Mary Magdalene. TIM: For example, there was an article

Blessed are the peacemakers: for they shall be called sons of God.

reason being that he wanted to work from only one established perspective,
the Bible is about as established as you can get.

The Overture is basically an electronic piece which cannot help but effect the
ner physically when played at the proper volume. It takes only about thirty
onds before you are taken into the music, and it doesn't let go of you until
final chords of the Crucifixion. The main reasons for this are the great
ety of musical themes plus the judicious use of their repetition. There is
ays just enough of what has come before to enable the listener to retain his
pective.

Although Christ is obviously the main character, it is Judas as the protagonist
has the pivotal role. The composers assure me that in live production this
ld be balanced by Christ's presence on stage. Nevertheless, it is Judas who
the mood of the story with an opening song (aria?):

Jesus! You've started to believe
The things they say of you
You really do believe
This talk of God is true
And all the good you've done
Will soon be swept away
You've begun to matter more
Than all the things you say

s Tim Rice explains it, "the movement had gotten out of hand" and Judas
doing only what he thought he had to do.

he apostles are introduced next, and they are portrayed almost as a bunch
ind followers who are looking forward only to retiring and writing the
els. We are then introduced to Mary Magdalene who, although historically a
re, comes off very much like a groupie whose only ambition is to care for
ired Christ. Yvonne Elliman, who sounds like a cross between Mary Hopkin
Linda Ronstadt, does an outstanding job with the character in two songs,
rything's Alright" and "I Don't Know How to Love Him", both the words
element is not established in Judas' opening song, it is very clearly established

fter some arguments with the priests to the effect that Jesus must die, we
the entrance into Jerusalem. Although Andrew Webber insists that the
c here is strongly derivitive of Prokofiev, it still sounds more to me like
thing Bizet might have omitted from CARMEN. The "Hosanna" is a march
h becomes to infective that after you've heard it a few times, you find your-
valking around humming the tune. It has much the same effect as the
mphal March" from AIDA, for example.

ollowing Christ's confrontation with the citizens of Jerusalem and a short

New York Sunday Times very recently in which the writer protested
ut the sexual implications, but if he and the people who also said
would read the lyrics, they would see that in the last verse Yvonne
s "Yet if he said he loved me, I'd be lost, I'd be frightened, I'd turn

Blessed are they that have been persecuted for righteousness' sake:

interlude of Pilate's dream, we have the scene in which Jesus throws the mon lenders out of the temple. It is at the conclusion of this scene that the prima musical theme is established. It is the theme which is to be used for the praye in Gethsemane and for the "Finale" immediately following the Crucifixion.

Once again it is Mary Magdalene who soothes Jesus following the money-lenders incident with the "I Don't Know How to Love Him" ballad. The scen then shifts to Judas who is plotting the betrayal with Caliaphas and Annas. A he is telling the soldiers where to find Christ, we have the only real hint of religious music in the whole piece with an angelic kind of chorus intoning, "V done Judas/Good old Judas."

Following an interchange between Christ and Judas during which Judas ac that he will betray Christ (this episode departs from the Biblical version sligh but as Tim Rice pointed out, Judas would not have been the kind of man no stand up when accused), the apostles exit very much content with themselve and warmed by the wine inside them. Jesus is left alone in the garden to pray and the theme is the one introduced in the moneylenders scene.

I have not mentioned thus far that Jesus Christ is played by Ian Gillan, wh the lead singer for Deep Purple. It is the kind of thing that you suspect that 1 Lehrer might have written:

"So you are the Christ/you're the great Jesus Christ
Prove to me that you're no fool/walk across my swimming pool
If you do that for me/then I'll let you go free
C'mon King of the Jews."

The change in musical forms is so drastic (but appropriate), that I asked And Webber about the song. His reply was that they needed a break in the drama is certainly that), and they also thought that the song was appropriate for He character. He went on to add that he saw Herod on the stage as a fat, balding man surrounded by a bevy of half-naked girls and puffing on a joint. And ho perfect.

Side Four begins with Judas' death and included a reprise of Mary's "I Do Know How to Love Him" sung by Judas. It is a clever piece of theatricality which the authors take an obvious delight in having employed. It's a little to of Broadway which works very well without being at all intrusive. An interes aside on the reprise is that it was included originally because Murray Head w plays Judas (again, brilliantly, I might add) liked the song and wanted to be to sing it. So it was added here, and the choice was a very good one.

Next we have Jesus' sentencing before Pilate during which we discover th Pilate was also human; he is having Christ crucified only because he apparent

my head, I'd back away". There is no affair, this is in black and on the record and in the show and....FROST: What is their relatio in Jesus Christ Superstar? TIM: The way I see it, I should kr suppose (laughter), Mary is in love with Jesus and for the first tin

as no choice. This scene also includes the "Thirty-Nine Lashes" sequence which ay be one of the few places where the composers over-indulged themselves. ne sequence is nothing more than an extended crescendo relying primarily on chestration for its power. While Andrew Webber's orchestrations are amazingly ventive, if occasionally derivitive (he admits to a strong Shostakovich influence), e lashed sequence does seem a bit tedious after a few listenings. But since that's e saying there's a fly speck on the Mona Lise, forget it.

The journey to Calvary is musically interpreted with the "Superstar" theme hich introduced the work about a year ago. It is sung by the offstage voice of das and generally summarizes the entire thesis of the opera:

"Jesus Christ, Jesus Christ
Who are you? What have you sacrificed?
Do you think you're what they say you are?"

ne questions asked in those four lines are essentially what the opera is all about. ut it is important to remember that you don't have to get hung up on those estions to enjoy the opera. And yes; you can even dance to it.

JESUS CHRIST SUPERSTAR concludes with a brief, obligatory Crucifixion ene and then a very gentle summation (emphasis on the strings) of the ethsemane theme. These last six minutes are a bit like coming off the last hill a musical roller coaster. There isn't too much excitement, but without them, ou'd be left suspended. I'm not sure that this isn't a weakness and that the ucifixion shouldn't have been explored a little further musically. But the point that the ending works, and that's really good enough.

Altogether, the opera runs just over eighty-seven minutes, and it is worth ery second of your attention. I am generally not one to come right out and commend that you go out and buy a record, but I will make an exception here. out and buy this record. At worst, it will entertain you; at best, it will amaze ou, and you will find yourself playing it over and over and dragging people in f the street to hear it. And that's as it should be.

The importance of JESUS CHRIST SUPERSTAR is not to be minimized. If ndrew Webber and Tim Rice ever realize their production in a theatre or on m, the opera stands to change the entire structure and future of modern music. l of the old conventions will be discarded (and it is past time for that to ppen) and we will have a music, call it rock if you like, which is finally worthy some respect from ALL levels. We have something right now that can be tened to and enjoyed by everyone from Milton Cross to Jimmy Page. And that one is quite an accomplishment.

in love with somebody mentally, previously it has been sort of ysical love....and there's been absolutely no contact at all.... NDREW: Surely, I mean the way I read the Bible was that Jesus was e of the very few people who actually regarded someone like Mary

A city set on a hill cannot be hid.

they hear"

Andrew Webber and Tim Rice originally conceived the idea from an extend
musical work on Christ as far back as six years ago, but nothing jelled until abc
eighteen months ago when they wrote and produced the single "Superstar" to
test the validity of their project. When the single sold over 100,000 copies, the
felt they had enough to go ahead. So after 18 months of work and over 400 ho
of recording sessions, the package has arrived.

For now, Webber and Rice have put aside any thoughts of further writing ir
campaign to get their opera produced on stage. They are being very careful abc
finding a backer, because they want to retain artistic control over the package.

One game that people are starting to play is casting the roles for the produc
tion. The composers have already said that they would probably retain Murray
Head as Judas and Barry Dennen as Pilate. But many people have already specu
lated about the rest of the cast, suggest that John Lennon would make a perfect Christ against Mick Jagger's Judas (Webber says that it would have to be tl
other way around because of Jagger's stage presence), but, in truth, the composers' choice for Christ is none other than Bob Dylan.

Now think about that while you're on the way to the record store to pick u
a copy of JESUS CHRIST SUPERSTAR—potentially the single most importan
recording since Edison waxed his first cylinder.

as worth talking to and I think we make that point very clearly...
think Tim does....TIM: He had a frightening effect on her, she was
absolutely baffled, I mean, here was this man who she was absolu
obsessed by and she didn't know why and her song ends "He scare:

Let your light shine before men.

love him so" and there is no affair. I think that this is....FROST: I can see that, it says here "I never thought I'd come to this, what's about yet if he said he loved me, I'd be lost". However, I think on tage they could....on the stage production, they could have had an

Glorify your Father which is in heaven.

BO**FE**

HOPE

FAITH

TRUST

SEEK

LYING

UNBELIEF

No miracles

ASK

PROTECTION

Mr. Give

Mr. Grab

GREAT

STEALING

GOD'S WORK

LITTLE

FIGHTING

Filled with wrath

"Thou hast hidden these things from the wise and understanding and revealed them to babes"

affair, I mean, this line could just mean "Yet if he said he loved
you know, we're having an affair, but if he had got to saying
TIM: Well, if they really were, I mean....anybody....FROST: Do
know what I mean, I'm not saying that's what's in your mi

Healing of the Centurion's Servant.

ALL
   He is dangerous

PRIEST 2
   The man is in town right now to whip up some support

PRIEST 3
   A rabble rousing mission that I think we must abort

ALL
   He is dangerous!

MOB outside
   Jesus Christ Superstar!

ALL
   He is dangerous!

PRIEST 2
   Look Caiaphas—they're right outside our yard

PRIEST 3
   Quick Caiaphas—go call the Roman guard

CAIAPHAS
   No wait—we need a more permanent solution
      to our problem...

ANNAS
   What then to do about Jesus of Nazareth
   Miracle wonderman—hero of fools?

PRIEST 3
   No riots, no army, no fighting, no slogans

TIM: No. No. No. FROST: But the way it's done on the stage, the
relationship is very....TIM: Oh, people with a certain type of mind....
could read anything into anything if they want to and I'm sure, you
now....(laughter and clapping)....FROST: Now we're delighted to

Raising of the Widow's Son.

CAISPHAS
One thing I'll say for him—Jesus is cool

ANNAS
We dare not leave him to his own devices
His half-witted fans will get out of control

PRIEST 3
But how can we stop him? His glamour increases
By leaps every minute—he's top of the poll

CAIAPHAS
I see bad things arising—the crowd crown him king
Which the Romans would ban
I see blood and destruction, our elimination
    because of one man
Blood and destruction because of one man

ALL
Because, because, because of one man

CAIAPHAS
Our elimination because of one man

ALL
Because, because, because of one, 'cause of one,
    'cause of one man

PRIEST 3
What then to do about this Jesusmania?

ANNAS
How do we deal with the carpenter king?

PRIEST 3
Where do we start with a man who is bigger
Than John was when John did his Baptism thing?

introduce to sing precisely that song we were just talking about, the
song 'I don't know how to love him', the lady who in fact sings it in the
show, and what a....and she gives a marvellous performance, I think, in
the show, don't you? ANDREW: Well absolutely. FROST: A marvellous

Message from the Baptist.

The Pope's own private radio station will broadcast, in full, the controversial "Jesus Christ/Superstar" rock opera, which is the story of the last seven days of Christ's life.

Radio Vatican will present two special programs of the best selling Decca album with comments by its two authors Tim Rice and Andrew Lloyd Webber which will be taken from a previously recorded interview with the young writers by some Roman Catholic dignitaries.

A spokesman for the Pope's private radio station said, "Nothing like this has ever been broadcast on Radio Vatican until now, but we feel that this is a work of considerable importance."

Tim Rice said: "When we contemplated Jesus Christ Superstar, we thought that there might be resistance in Roman Catholic countries. But oddly enough it has been better received there than in some of the Church of England areas. We think that it must be that they have heightened awareness of religious subjects—as opposed to what can only be described as apathy in England."

performance as Mary Magdalene in the show, will you welcome Yvonne Elliman. I don't know how to love him. FROST: Welcome back with Andrew and Tim who you met earlier and Yvonne who we just met.... That was beautiful Yvonne, thank you very much indeed, lovely....How

Visit to Simon the Pharisee.

"A prophet is not w

Parable of the Two Debtors.

thout honour except

ou're not from London though are you? YVONNE: No, I'm from
awaii. FROST: Hawaii! (Cheers) YVONNE: But I went to London....
eah....FROST: Our audience came from all over the world just to be
ere this evening, yes, the....YVONNE: And I'm singing in that Club

The Ministering Women of Galilee.

in his own country

with my guitar and Andrew walked in and after the show, he came
to me and he said "You're my Mary Magdalene". O.K. and I didn't kno
who she was and he started talking about Jesus Christ and I though
you know, a Jesus freak, you know, and I guess he's going to do an albu

Controversy with the Pharisees.

Annunziata Parish
City of Ladue
Missouri

Decca Records, Inc.
445 Park Avenue
New York, N.Y. 10022

Gentlemen:

I am asking the members of my parish
to stop buying any Decca records. I
will also encourage them to persuade
their friends to do likewise. Your
record, "Jesus Christ, Superstar" by
Biff Rose is an insult to all Christians.

Sincerely yours,

Rt. Rev. James R. Hartnett
Pastor, Annunziata Parish

Whom It May Concern:

writing in reference to your album "Jesus Christ Superstar". I thought you
re a very reputable Company but anyone that has to stoop that low as to use
r Lord's name to make money is no better than the scum of the earth. I never
ard the album nor would I waste hard earned money to listen to it.

u probably think that as long as you can get the young of our country to fall
r it you've got it made. Well you might make your money now but later on
en your company falls flat on its face remember back years ago when you
d our Lord's name to get where you are. Sooner or later you will have to pay
this.

enough of us get together maybe we can stop you now. I would like an
olanation as to why you recorded this if you feel you have one.

cerely,

s. Catherine Hirst
sington, Pa. 19029

dn't really know what it was all about. I went in and I sang the song
had an instant hit, you know. FROST: Incredible, yes and the
ment you....did Andrew have to explain to you about who....who
lained to you about Mary Magdalene. YVONNE: Yeah, well, one

The Sower.

The Church of God in Arkansas
304 Oaklawn Blvd.
Hot Springs, Arkansas

The President Of
Decca Record Company
445 Park Avenue,
New York, N.Y.

The "love of money", Mr. President; is the root of all evil, so the Word of God
tells us. It seems that there is literally nothing men deem wrong in their mad
rush to obtain wealth.

I am shocked that a recording company would stoop so low to blaspheme the
Holy name of God's own son. I'm sure you know that I am referring to your
record, "SUPERSTAR". Mr. President, there are laws in our country to protect
people from SLANDER. Jesus Christ is a Person. We Christians are not going to
sit on the sidelines and let His name be ridiculed in such fashion. My advice to
kooks like those whose lives are patterned after everything that is vile, vulgar
and profane, is to use their brain, as hard as it may be, and turn from their evil
ways before they wake up in HELL!

Mr. President, if you have legal counsel, I would advise you to seek it for we
plan to STOP this type of thing PERMANENTLY! We are thinking of sueing
your company and the Trinidad Singers for $10,000,000 each! How does that
set with YOU?

See You in Court,

Billy Landers
Minister of Oaklawn Church of God

P.S.   I suppose you have heard that our number one radio station has banned
ALL DECCA records because of this one vile recording.

day when I was doing the song I asked him, you know, who she w
I thought, you see....Mary, the only Mary I could relate to was Je
mother, and so I thought I was Jesus' mother, you know. The s
didn't quite make it with the lyrics (laughter)....so I found out who

"Love your enemies, bless them that curse you, do good to them that hate you,

s. I really don't know that much about her, I would like to know ore, if anybody could possibly tell me. FROST: Did you have a go at ading the Bible, or not? YVONNE: I looked and I scanned through e Bible and I tried to find Mary Magdalene and they just had the

The kingdom of heaven is likened unto a man

and pray for them which despitefully use you, and persecute you"

same thing written in every place. ANDREW: Especially as M
Magdalene doesn't....itn't really mentioned, I mean, a phenome
amount. TIM: And there's conflicting views in the Gospel as to exac
who she was, when, where and everything. FROST: I was, I was j

that sowed good seed in his field:

AIAPHAS
Fools! You have no perception!
The stakes we are gambling are frighteningly high!
We must crush him completely—
So like John before him, this Jesus must die
For the sake of the nation this Jesus must die

LL
Must die, must die, this Jesus must die

AIAPHAS
So like John before him, this Jesus must die

LL
Must die, must die, this Jesus must, Jesus must,
   Jesus must die!

HOSANNA

ROWD

osanna Heysanna Sanna Sanna Ho
Sanna Hey Sanna Ho Sanna
Hey JC, JC won't you smile at me?
Sanna Ho Sanna Hey Superstar

AIAPHAS
Tell the rabble to be quiet we anticipate a riot
This common crowd is much too loud
Tell the mob who sing your song that they are fools
   and they are wrong
They are a curse, they should disperse

ROWD
Hosanna Heysanna Sanna Sanna Ho
Sanna Hey Sanna Ho Sanna
Hey JC, JC you're alright by me
Sanna Ho Sanna Hey Superstar

inking that's an intriguing thought, though, that lyric sung by Mary,
e mother of Jesus, isn't is. That....that would be a new interpretation
 the part too. YVONNE: That'd cause a scandal, I could tell you.
ROST: Yes it really....what....what reaction have you had? I mean

but while men slept, his enemy came

Why waste your breath moaning at the crowd?
Nothing can be done to stop the shouting
If every tongue was still the noise would still continue
The rocks and stones themselves would start to sing:

CROWD (with JESUS)
Hosanna Heysanna Sanna Sanna Ho
Sanna Hey Sanna Ho Sanna
Hey JC, JC won't you fight for me?
Sanna Ho Sanna Hey Superstar

SIMON ZEALOTES

CROWD
Christ you know I love you
Did you see I waved?
I believe in you and God
So tell me that I'm saved
Christ you know I love you
Did you see I waved?
I believe in you and God
So tell me that I'm saved
Jesus I am with you
Touch me touch me Jesus
Jesus I am on your side
Kiss me kiss me Jesus

SIMON ZEALOTES
Christ, what more do you need to convince you
That you've made it and you're easily as strong
As the filth from Rome who rape our country
And who've terrorized our people for so long?

have you had any special reaction because you are dealing in
special religious material, I mean, do you find people react to you
different way, I mean, do people expect you to have religious pow
or things like that, or supernatural powers. YVONNE: Well, peo

and sowed tares, also among the wheat,

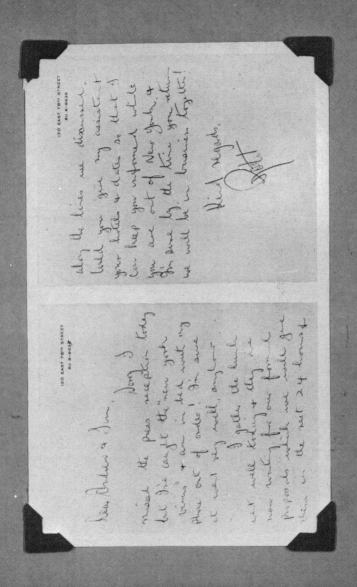

things like that, or supernatural powers? YVONNE: Well, people
e reacted to me sort of sexually, in a way, you know, thinking that
the Mary Magdalene type and I tell them, you know, it's all an
...Some people come to me....I did a show with a concert tour....

and went away.

David Laud
→

went to Chatanooga, and a couple of chicks came up to me afte
concert and said "My girl friend's in the hospital and she's been para
you know, from the neck down and she would really love to see yo
I thought, oh, I'm tired and, you know, and like this was what

The kingdom of heaven is like unto leaven.

Andrew ←

David Shaw (of RSO) ←

ng and I said I'll try and find some other people to go with you,
now, because I really want to get some sleep and I went to people
obody wanted to go and so I thought oh well I might as well go
went there and this girl, I touched her and she thought she could

He that soweth the good seed is the Son of man;

Colour captions 'Superstar' on Broadway

Right—Yvonne Elliman as Mary and Jeff Fenholt as Jesus

Overleaf—'Hosanna Heysanna Sanna Sanna Ho'

Left—'Prove to me that you're no fool Walk across my swimming pool'

Final Colour Photo—'Father into your hands I commend my spirit'

feel me and she had so much hope in her eyes and she get very st
all of a sudden, she said I know this is a sign, you know, and it
made me feel so good, I mean, people actually having me con
touch them and to be with them just to raise their spirits up. You k

and the field is the world,

8 Lessey Street
nherst, Mass 01002

ar Sirs:

is letter is in reference to an album on your label, "Jesus Christ Superstar."
vould like to say that it is in many ways the finest record ever made.
usically its great, and as a religious work it far surpasses the Bible.

ncerely,

rry Rhodes

cca Records
Division of MCA, Inc.
5 Park Avenue
w York City
w York 10022

ntlemen:

is is to request your permission to
nscribe the below listed booklet
o braille for Miss Donna Siren of
s city, and to hold the master copy
d make it available for duplication
r other blind persons anywhere in
e world who might want a copy in
aille.

SUS CHRIST, SUPERSTAR
XSA—7206)

e provide the braille copy of this
oklet free to Miss Siren and to any
her blind person asking for a copy.
ur work is done by volunteers.

If you receive requests for this booklet in braille, you may forward them
to us and we will be happy to send a
copy to any blind person free of
charge.

Your immediate response to this
request will be appreciated so that we
can transcribe this booklet for Miss
Siren as soon as possible. Thank you.

Sincerely,

Victor S. Hemphill,
Coordinator

OST: That's incredible, don't....YVONNE: But it was a nice thing
me, let me tell you I felt great....FROST: Does that happen a lot,
people actually come back stage and hope for a miracle? ANDREW:
n't really know, I mean, probably....Yvonne is probably better able

and the good seed, these are the sons of the kingdom;

331 Dunglison
University of Virginia
Charlottesville, Virginia 22905

Dear Sir,

 I would like to have permission to use the music from Andrew Lloyd Webb
and Tim Rice's "Jesus Christ, Superstar" to cut a record for our University's A
American basketball candidate, Barry Parkhill.

 All profits from this venture will go to the University of Virginia's Athletic
Scholarship program. The record being primarily a promotional idea, and since
these profits that are made will go to a worthy cause, would it be possible to
waive the royalty fees normally stipulated. A full financial account of the reco
would be made available to you, and I would consider this letter as a binding
agreement.

 As the basketball season is only a few months long, I would appreciate any
thing you can do to speed up the legal processes.

 Thank you for your time, consideration, and efforts.

 Sincerely,

 Robert Ainsley Hilliard

THE BALLAD OF BARRY PARKHILL

Words by R. Ainsley Hilliard
Music from Andrew Lloyd Webber's and Tim Rice's "Jesus Christ, Superstar"

BARRY PARKHILL . . . SUPERSTAR!!
THE ALL-AMERICAN THAT THEY SAY YOU ARE!

BARRY PARKHILL . . . CAVALIER!!
YOU AND THE WAHOOS IN THEIR FINEST YEAR!

Everytime they talk about the best in the sport,
Wahoo fans see Barry dribbling down the court.

Jump shots, defense, passing that just cannot be topped.
You're the one Atlantic Coast guard rivals can't stop.

Word of your great talents will reach the whole nation.
You just have to be the greatest A.C.C. sensation.

  Don't you get us wrong . . . We already know . . .
  Well, he's number one . . . He's just the very best . . .

to sort of say that than I am. YVONNE: Yeah, we get a lot of
strange people, you know. I mean it's really quite enchanting, you
cripples and things like that coming to concerts. FROST: That's e
ordinary. I didn't realise that. YVONNE: And, eh, I don't know r

and the tares are the sons of the evil one;

BARRY PARKHILL ... SUPERSTAR!!
THE ALL-AMERICAN THAT THEY SAY YOU ARE!

BARRY PARKHILL ... CAVALIER!!
YOU AND THE WAHOOS IN THEIR FINEST YEAR!

Coaches, writers, who d'ya think's the pick of the crop?
Tell us all the players that will get to the top.

Teams around the A.C.C., well what is their fate?
Other schools, now do they have the players that rate?

Come to U.Va. and see the best show in town.
Mr. B.P. tops them all; the best guard around.

> Don't you get us wrong ... We already know ...
> Well, he's number one ... He's just the very best ...

REFRAIN

MCA MUSIC

445 PARK AVENUE, NEW YORK, N. Y. 10022, TEL. (212) PLAZA 9-7500
LEEDS MUSIC CORPORATION • DUCHESS MUSIC CORPORATION • PICKWICK MUSIC
NORTHERN MUSIC CORPORATION • CHAMPION MUSIC CORPORATION • HAWAII MUSIC COMPANY, INC.

16th December 1971

Mr. Robert A. Hilliard
331 Dunglison
University of Virginia
Charlottesville, Va. 22905.

Dear Mr. Hilliard,

Thank you for your letter of the 14th requesting permission to record a parody version of the title song
from the rock opera JESUS CHRIST SUPERSTAR. We
must, however, deny your request since our contract
with the writers expressly prohibits any parody versions.

Thank you for your interest.

Sincerely,

John McKellan

sb

to react to these things except to just say that, you know, I'm not
y Magdalene, but Yvonne Elliman, but, you know, touch me if you
t to and you know, be happy, and whatever....It's really part of the
FROST: That's really the only way to handle it. ANDREW: I

and the enemy that sowed them is the devil;

18 Clarke Court
Sharon, Mass.

Dear Sirs:

I am fourteen years old and live in Sharon, Mass. A group of fourteen year olds and myself would very much like to put on a performance of your rock opera "Jesus Christ Superstar." We would like to do this for several reasons. Firstly we would charge about fifty cents per ticket for admission. This money would go to the Pakistan Relief Program. Secondly we think this would be a lot of fun and extremely good drama and music education.

We would not wish to purchase scripts, for many of us have the booklet which comes with the record and we would only want to do the songs. We will have several adults working with us. Could you please tell me how much it would cost us in royalties? Could you please send this information as quickly as possible.

Sincerely,

Jodi Rafkin

wonder if it happens to people who are playing other things, I m
because, I mean this is not the only, by any means, you know, the o
thing that has been written about Christ, I mean, there have been ot
since we started writing and it would be interesting to know, I m

and the harvest is the end of the world;

hrist you know I love you
id you see I waved?
believe in you and God
o tell me that I'm saved
hrist you know I love you
id you see I waved?
believe in you and God
o tell me that I'm saved
esus I am with you
ouch me touch me Jesus
sus I am on your side
iss me kiss me Jesus

ION ZEALOTES

here must be over fifty thousand
creaming love and more for you
veryone of fifty thousand
Vould do whatever you ask him to
eep them yelling their devotion
ut add a touch of hate at Rome
ou will rise to a greater power
Ve will win ourselves a home
ou'll get the power and the glory
or ever and ever and ever
men! Amen!

POOR JERUSALEM

SUS

either you Simon, nor the fifty thousand
Nor the Romans, nor the Jews, nor Judas nor the Twelve,
Nor the Priests, nor the Scribes

n to opera singers and things, whether people who are very much
ved by music, Bach's Saint Matthew Passion or something, whether
ple are even moved by music to that extent. FROST: Yes and it
ald be interesting...fascinating thought that people do, I mean, it's

and the reapers are angels.

Understand what power is
Understand what glory is
Understand at all... understand at all
If you knew all that I knew, my poor Jerusalem
You'd see the truth, but you close your eyes
But you close your eyes
While you live your troubles are many, poor Jerusalem
To conquer death you only have to die
You only have to die

PILATE'S DREAM

Pontius Pilate's house, Monday

PILATE

dreamed I met a Galilean
He had that look you very rarely find
A most amazing man
The haunting hunted kind

I asked him to say what had happened
How it all began
I asked again—he never said a word
As if he hadn't heard

And next the room was full of wild and angry men
They seemed to hate this man—they fell on him and then
They disappeared again

Then I saw thousands of millions
Crying for this man
And then I heard them mentioning my name
And leaving me the blame

partly attributed, I guess, to the power of the work, but also, to
you know, more I think to the power of people's association wi
with the whole Gospel story. YVONNE: Yeah. FROST: Sorry. T
was only going to say that this illustrates again the fact that, to a ce

As therefore the tares are gathered up and burned with fire;

St. Monica's Rectory
34 Monica Street
Rochester
New York 14619

Leeds Music Corporation
445 Park Avenue
New York, New York

Gentlemen:

I am writing to ask permission to put on a production of "Jesus Christ Superstar" in St. Monica's Church during Holy Week, (March 26—April 1).

The purpose is to try to put an end to divisions among the youth of this inner-city area. This could possible be the first time the Black, Red and White teenagers would work together and discover their common humanity. We have an adequate number of professional and semi-professional volunteers who would direct the students; technicians from local colleges would help with lighting and staging.

We would charge no admission. We have an extremely limited budget from local churches and community organisations and so we request exemption from royalties.

We will anxiously await your reply.

Sincerely,

Rev. Walter J. Hanss

P.S. If you can grant permission, could you please let us know where and how to get scripts and music?

xtent, it's got a bit out of control, I mean, two years ago we were just writing our first serious attempt at an opera and it ends up with sort of the people going to Yvonne to be healed, which is, I mean, completely not what you know, we imagined two years ago. The thing just has

so shall it be in the end of the world.

snowballed out of all proprotion, which, in a way, almost counts ag us at times, people sort of write reviews, you know, saying "I was disappointed here" and it's really a bit strange that two writers sh get the sort of word 'disappointed' in their first work, I mean, I m

The Son of man shall send forth his angels,

be if we'd had nineteen hit shows and the twentieth wasn't quite so
d, then you could say this. I was a bit disappointed. ANDREW: Yes,
even just one. YVONNE: But if it gives people hope you know, I
in that's good. I mean, this girl when she said it was a sign she felt

and they shall gather out of his kingdom

We wish to inform you that all MCA's offices will be closed on December 25th in observance of 'Superstar's' birthday

MCA advertisement

stronger and that can't be bad. FROST: If she really was stronger,
long as wasn't....ANDREW: When we first came to America a y
ago....a bit over a year ago now, we came, actually....we funnily enou
came over to see a production of our 'Joseph and the Amazing Tech

all things that cause stumbling,

our Dream Coat', which we wrote for children and was performed by me Catholic priests in Long Island....TIM: Yeah, Douglaston. NDREW: Douglaston, and....in their college and we came over there d we were sort of talking about the other, and I must say, we were

and them that do iniquity,

RECD.   JAN 1 5 1971

DATE __January 15, 1971__

TO _____Ellis Nassour_____ at _____

FROM __Tony Martell__ at_____

SUBJECT _____

Per your memo, you c
additional gold recc
SUPERSTAR for Tim Ri

You can also order c
Henry Brief send the
company. We will pa
requested by Tim Ric

Regards.

TM:tm

very pleased in a way that there has become, I mean, interest in Ch
because it seems to me a topic that's well worth discussing
particularly in England there hasn't been any interest really am
young people in Christ, or Christianity or religion at all until the

and shall cast them into the furnace of fire:

MUNICATION

	COPY TO	AT
	Herb Gordon	_____
_	Bill Levy	_____
_	Jack Loetz ✓	_____
_	_____	_____

ahead and have two
rds made up on

Stigwood, but have
directly to that
the two plaques

n this sort of reawakening in comparative religion which seems to be
y recent and I am very glad and happy about that. FROST: But, I
an, in fact, you wrote this ahead....people write Time cover stories
so on about the Jesus revolution, but in fact, that's really some-

there shall be the weeping and gnashing of teeth.

"The initial pressing was 100,000 but I put in an order for another hundred because I can't remember when I've ever believed more in a product."

Tony Martell Vice President (Merchandising)

"The initial pressing was 100,000 but I put in an order for another hundred because I can't remember when I've ever believed more in a product."

Tony Martell Vice President (Merchandising)

"The initial pressing was 100,000 but I put in an order for another hundred because I can't remember when I've ever believed more in a product."

Tony Martell Vice President (Merchandising)

"The initial pressing was 100,000 but I put in an order for another hundred because I can't remember when I've ever believed more in a product."

Tony Martell Vice President (Merchandising)

"The initial pressing was 100,000 but I put in an order for another hundred because I can't remember when I've ever believed more in a product."

Tony Martell Vice President (Merchandising)

"The initial pressing was 100,000 but I put in an order for another hundred because I can't remember when I've ever believed more in a product."

Tony Martell Vice President (Merchandising)

"The initial pressing was 100,000 but I put in an order for another hundred because I can't remember when I've ever believed more in a product."

Tony Martell Vice President (Merchandising)

"The initial pressing was 100,000 but I put in an order for another hundred because I can't remember when I've ever believed more in a product."

Tony Martell Vice President (Merchandising)

"The initial pressing was 100,000 but I put in an order for another hundred because I can't remember when I've ever believed more in a product."

Tony Martell Vice President (Merchandising)

"The initial pressing was 100,000 but I put in an order for another hundred because I can't remember when I've ever believed more in a product."

Tony Martell Vice President (Merchandising)

"The initial pressing was 100,000 but I put in an order for another hundred because I can't remember when I've ever believed more in a product."

Tony Martell Vice President (Merchandising)

"The initial pressing was 100,000 but I put in an order for another hundred because I can't remember when I've ever believed more in a product."

Tony Martell Vice President (Merchandising)

"I mean Decca hadn't had a hit in 100 years so when they got this they just ran with it"

Barry Kittleson

thing that last year, in fact, you'd written Jesus Christ Superstar already in fact. TIM: Yes, it was all a coincidence, I mean, um....we just had t come out at the right time, I mean, timing's everything, we're the fir to admit that the success of the record is probably 75% luck, I mean, w

Then shall the righteous shine forth

THE TEMPLE

MONEYLENDERS AND MERCHANTS

Roll on up—for my price is down
Come on in—for the best in town
Take your pick of the finest wine
Lay your bets on this bird of mine
Roll on up—for my price is down
Come on in—for the best in town
Take your pick of the finest wine
Lay your bets on this bird of mine
Name your price I got everything
Come and buy it's all going fast
Borrow cash on the finest terms
Hurry now while stocks still last.

JESUS

My temple should be a house of prayer
But you have made it a den of thieves
Get out! Get out!
My time is almost through
Little left to do
After all I've tried for three years, seems like thirty
Seems like thirty

CROWD

See my eyes I can hardly see
See me stand I can hardly walk
I believe you can make me whole
See my tongue I can hardly talk
See my skin I'm a mass of blood
See my legs I can hardly stand
I believe you can make me well
See my purse I'm a poor poor man

think it's a good record, but if it had come out, say five years
lier, or even now, um....it wouldn't have done half as well purely
cause we just happen to hit the right time....FROST: When did it....
M: It was unintentional. ANDREW: Right. FROST: We're in fact

as the sun in the kingdom of their Father.

Won't you touch will you mend me Christ
Won't you touch will you heal me Christ
Will you kiss you can cure me Christ
Won't you kiss won't you pay me Christ

There's too many of you—don't push me
There's too little of me—don't crowd me
Heal yourselves!

EVERYTHING'S ALRIGHT

MARY MAGDALENE

Try not to get worried try not to turn on to
Problems that upset you oh don't you know
Everything's alright yes everything's fine

JESUS

And I think I shall sleep well tonight
Let the world turn without me tonight

MARY MAGDALENE

Close your eyes close your eyes
And forget all about us tonight

I DON'T KNOW HOW TO LOVE HIM

MARY MAGDALENE

I don't know how to love him
What to do how to move him
I've been changed yes really changed
In these past few days when I've seen myself
I seem like someone else

I don't know how to take this
I don't see why he moves me

going to hear now another song from the show Jesus Christ Supers
can you tell us where this song comes and tell us a bit about how y
wrote it....TIM: This is 'Everything's all right', I take it?....FROS
Yes it is, tell us a little bit about how you....TIM: Well, this is a ve

He that hath ears, let him hear.

Dear Sole Selling Agents of Jesus Christ
   Superstar, namely Leeds Music Corporation
   With a start like this you probably
want to know what I want. It's a short
story so I start at the begining. I'm a
junior in high school and I happen to be
in a second year drama class. As a opps!
second semester assignment, we're to
chose a play, hack it up (cut it) and present a 30 minute readers theatre. After
some thought I decided to try my luck
and present Jesus Christ Superstar (I
wouldn't be writing you if I were going
to do something else, now would I!!).
Any way the thought popped into my
my to secure copyright permission (I
live near Kansas City, Mo. and hassle
arose this summer over some people
who were going to prerfsent J.C.S. opps!
without you're permission, they got into
all sorts of trouble (I don't want to)
My prentation will be about 30 minutes
and I'll only do for my drama class,
(no charge or anything like that, just
in a class room situation) so I am
wondering if I can have permission
to do it and not have to pay royalty
                                    (over)

mple song, it's a ballad, it's a lullaby really I suppose, it's a....and it's
recurring theme which we hope works because it is very simple and
s sung by Yvonne both to Judas and to Christ during their first
gument and she's just trying to calm things down and say 'Everything's

The kingdom of heaven is like unto a treasure hidden in the field:

because somthing tells me that the royalty for J.C.S. is expensive and I am not rich. So if it isn't a lot of trouble I'd like to know in a few days.

Thankyou
very much,
Renee Holland
7207 Overton
Raytown, Mo.
64133

P.S. Even if I get your permission I'm not sure I'll get to do Superstar any way. oops! You see my drama teacher is the wife of a Baptist minister and don't think she appreciates Superstar the way I do. Three-fourths of the fight with be to win her over. Anyway thanks again and I'll let you know what happens.

all right, don't worry.', when of course it obviously isn't. Things a going headlong, you know, towards the Crucifixion. FROST: Wou you sing that for us now, Yvonne....lovely....FROST: Now we're bac with Tim and Andrew and Yvonne, thank you very much inde

which a man found and hid;

that he was not aware that he was infringing and that such infringement could not have been reasonably foreseen; and

(d) To perform or represent the copyrighted work publicly if it be a drama or, if it be a dramatic work and not reproduced in copies for sale, to vend any manuscript or any record whatsoever thereof; to make or to procure the making of any transcription or record thereof by or from which, in whole or in part, it may in any manner or by any method be exhibited, performed, represented, produced, or reproduced; and to exhibit, perform, represent, produce, or reproduce it in any manner or by any method whatsoever; and

(e) To perform the copyrighted work publicly for profit if it be a musical composition; and for the purpose of public performance for profit, and for the purposes set forth in subsection (a) hereof, to make any arrangement or setting of it or of the melody of it in any system of notation or any form of record in which the thought of an author may be recorded and from which it may be read or reproduced: *Provided*, That the provisions of this title, so far as they secure copyright controlling the parts of instruments serving to reproduce mechanically the musical work, shall include only compositions published and copyrighted after July 1, 1909, and shall not include the works of a foreign author or composer unless the foreign state or nation of which such author or composer is a citizen or subject grants, either by treaty, convention, agreement, or law, to citizens of the United States similar rights. And as a ...echanical ...right has ...the copy- ...reproduce ...ake simi- ...copyright ...ufactured, ...right pro- ...furnish, a ...umber of ...us month ...nd royal- ...ny month ...ent of the ...rticles or ...er contri- ...nance for ...e uses the ...rts of in-

NOTICE

This will notify whoever may be concerned that no performances of JESUS CHRIST SUPERSTAR may be held without prior written authorization from the Robert Stigwood Organisation Ltd., 67 Brook Street, London W.1, England

So far no licenses have been granted to perform JESUS CHRIST SUPERSTAR to any persons whomsoever

vonne. The....has, has your views, for instance, changed the time ou've been how long have you been associated with Jesus Christ Super ar? YVONNE: A year and a half, two years....FROST: Have you.... ve your views on Jesus Christ or God altered in that time, or not....?

and in his joy he goeth and selleth all that he hath,

J.B., a record-industry mogul: "You all know why we're here."

Staff: Right, J.B."

"Religion is in, protest out, Right?"

"Right, J.B."

"We have to move fast. We can't do the seven last days of Christ, because those English kids beat us to it with J.C. Superstar. We can't do a Mass, because Lenny Bernstein's got that market cornered. But that's the kind of product I'm after. I want a heavenly voice, and I want message."

"Well, J.B., we have here a property called the Messiah. It's got everything going for it, starting with a steady, 230-year track record. It has a Christmas section and—get this—an Easter section too. How can we miss? And listen. There's a Pastoral Symphony for the country-and-western crowd. Set it to rock and—"

"Boys and girls, I buy it. Just keep the beat and the chord changes simple. And don't forget to put a cross on the jacket cover."

That probably is not the way the new RCA rock version of Handel's "Messiah" came into being—but one wonders. Rarely has so much conceit, commercial cynicism, bad taste, musical ignorance and all-round incompetence been brought together within the grooves of a single LP. Written and arranged by Producer David Axelrod (Electric Prunes), conducted by the jazz world's Cannonball Adderley, the RCA "Messiah" has something to offend everyone.

—TIME

YVONNE: Well, I certainly know a lot more about the man, a don't know how to accept Him as of yet, you know, I ah....He, He gives, He makes me have a very good feeling, I've had a lot of ru when I was doing a concert where I've felt God's presence there

and buyeth that field.

know, it was incredible....introducing me and I'm getting it slowly
maybe some day, I'll accept it, you know accept Him as my Saviour,
thing could happen. FROST: What, what, what....how certain are
h of you, you said that Jesus Christ Super Star is a question, you

The Storm on the Lake.

AMERICA ROCK OPERA COMPANY PRESENTS
A SYMPHONIC ROCK CONCERT
FEATURING 1½ HOURS OF MUSIC FROM
JESUS CHRIST SUPERSTAR
AND OTHER SELECTED WORKS

ONE PERFORMANCE ONLY
OVER 75 PERFORMERS WITH THE S.F. SYMPHONIC ORCHESTRA
SATURDAY   SEPTEMBER 25   8:30 P.M.
COW PALACE
TICKETS 4.50 5.50 6.50   ALL TICKETRON LOCATIONS   COW PALACE BOXOFFICE   ALL MACY'S LOCATIONS
S.F. DOWNTOWN CENTER BOXOFFICE   SAN JOSE BOXOFFICE   INFORMATION 334-4852

know, rather than an answer, do you have more answers now than whe
you wrote it? TIM: Not really, um....I suppose we have again, as Yvon
said, much more information, one's read much more since writing it a
when people write to us and, um, we often look up things they sugge

The Gerasene Demoniac.

read, you know, um....some suggest it forcibly, some, you know,
t suggest politely, um....I think really our attitude is, is more or less
e same that, that we are unable ourselves to see Christ as a God and
e see Him as a phenomenally remarkable man, a very inspiring man

The Healing of Jairus' Daughter.;

ravening wolves"

Recorded by
The National Rock Opera Company

and I think the story of Christ as a man is extremely relevant to toda
I mean, it's....just because it's such an inspiring story, um, and Sup
Star doesn't say that Christ is or isn't God, it doesn't categorically.
ANDREW: We purposely....TIM: Deny His divinity or assert

of the Woman with the Issue of Blood;

He's a man he's just a man
And I've had so many men before

In very many ways
He's just one more

Should I bring him down should I scream and shout
Should I speak of love let my feelings out
I never thought I'd come to this—what's it all about

Don't you think it's rather funny
I should be in this position
I'm the one who's always been
So calm so cool, no lover's fool
Running every show
He scares me so

I never thought I'd come to this—what's it all about
Yet if he said he loved me
I'd be lost I'd be frightened
I couldn't cope just couldn't cope
I'd turn my head I'd back away
I wouldn't want to know
He scares me so
I want him so
I love him so

DAMNED FOR ALL TIME
Tuesday

JUDAS

Now if I help you it matters that you see
These sordid kind of things are coming hard to me
It's taken me some time to work out what to do
I weighed the whole thing up before I came to you

ANDREW: We tried to avoid making the thing a personal actual statement, at no time do we make a personal statement. FROST: Is that why you ended it at the Crucifixion rather than going on to the resurrection which would instantly raise the point of whether He was...

and of Two Blind Men.

I have no thought at all about my own reward
I really didn't come here of my own accord
Just don't say I'm
Damned for all time

I came because I had to I'm the one who saw
Jesus can't control it like he did before
And furthermore I know that Jesus thinks so too
Jesus wouldn't mind that I was here with you
I have no thought at all about my own reward
I really didn't come here of my own accord
Just don't say I'm
Damned for all time

Annas you're a friend a wordly man and wise
Caiaphas my friend I know you sympathise
Why are we the prophets? Why are we the ones?
Who see the sad solution—know what must be done
I have no thought at all about my own reward
I really didn't come here of my own accord
Just don't say I'm
Damned for all time

ANNAS
Cut the protesting forget the excuses
We want information get up off the floor

CAIAPHAS
We have the papers we need to arrest him
You know his movements—we know the law

ANNAS
Your help in this matter won't go unrewarded

CAIAPHAS
We'll pay you in silver—cash on the nail
We just need to know where the soldiers can find him

ANDREW: Well I think it would do more than that, I think it wo
become very subjective, I mean, Tim and I, you know, are not entir
sure, as I expect none of us really would altogether agree about
Resurrection, I mean, because it can be looked at in so many ways a

Second Visit to Nazareth.

w York—Robert Stigwood, chairman of the Robert Stigwood Group Ltd., has
ued a warning to any and all persons who attempt to present the rock opera
esus Christ—Superstar" in concert or dramatic form, the copyrights to which
e solely owned by his organization, the composers Andrew Lloyd Webber and
m Rice, and Leeds Music Ltd.

Stigwood declared that he, the authors, publishers, "keenly sensitive to what
necessary to present this monumental work to the public in an artistic fashion,"
d arranged their own authorized concert tour, which will get underway on
y 12 in Pittsburgh. A company of 20 singers plus a 32-piece orchestra includ-
a rock band will be supervised by the authors, he added. The William Morris
ency is booking the tour through Oct. That month, a Broadway version opens
the Mark Hellinger Theatre.

Branding these parties "outright pirates," Stigwood said: "It is patently clear
t a small group of people have set out to mislead and deceive the public. We
end, in every case, to pursue vigorously anyone who attempts to infringe on
r copyrights."

Stigwood's attorneys, Eastman & Eastman, and Robert Osterberg of
eles and Clark have already successfully halted proposed productions of the
rk in Washington, D.C.; Baltimore, Richmond, Louisville, Cincinnati, New
leans, Memphis, Philadelphia, Cleveland, and St. Louis.

In Toronto, earlier last week, a judge ordered the Canadian Rock Opera Com-
ny to post a substantial bond and appointed an accountant to audit all monies
the production scheduled for June 27, pending a forthcoming trial. The judge
o ordered that the title 'Jesus Christ—Superstar' be removed from all adver-
ng of the concert.

There is presently outstanding a preliminary injunction in the U.S. District
urt, Southern District of New York, enjoining the American Rock Opera
mpany and other defendants from performing 'Superstar'. We have moved to
ite them for contempt of court on the grounds that they have violated Judge
nstance Baker Motley's previous injunction. This cast will be heard on Tuesday,
ne 29.

Stigwood said he has evidence that "these people have illegally advertised the
e of the work and pretended to the courts by saying they only wish to per-
m selections from the opera, whereas they have gone on to perform the entire
rk without any regard to the authors' rights. One company had the audacity
alter the work by adding a resurection scene. Yet another doctored the opera
adding The Lord's Prayer, as well as a currently popular contemporary song."

felt it would probably lose the, I don't know, the just sort of
tional impact of the story if we went on to that, I mean, it's not
ething... we're not the only person who...people who have stopped, I
n, as you know....FROST: No. ANDREW: I mean, Bach did and

Sending Forth of the Apostles.

it's just, I think, a....a....a very subjective, a very subjective area....T
Because basically the story of Christ the man and I feel that one of t
reasons why Christ has, sort of....hasn't been so sort of widely accep
in schools and with young people in recent years in England is becau

John the Baptist's Death.

Jesus Christ—Superstar

Pittsburgh, July 13.

Robert Stigwood in association with MCA Inc., by arrangement with David Land, presentation, featuring Carl Anderson, Jeff Fenholt, Yvonne Elliman, Frankie Madrid, Jim Turner, Bob Bingham, Phil Methro, Eric Mercury, Lyle Countryman, Susan Allanson, Mike Wade, Allen Martin, and the Randall's Island instrumental group; cast of 30 plus 32 piece orchestra. Musical Director Marc Pressel. Music by Andrew Lloyd Webber, lyrics by Tim Rice. World premiere, Civic Arena, July 12, 1971; $6 top.

Jesus Christ—Superstar", in its world premiere date and its first authorized showing, broke every existing record at the Civic Arena Monday (12) night, bringing in 13,640 persons for a gross of $66,262, topping the record set previously by Tom Jones last year when he brought in an audience of 13,323.

Outstanding from a trade point of view was the dominance of family groups in the audience. All ages were seen everywhere in the crowd.

The show's strength is also indicated by its big draw in the face of an 11-week-old newspaper strike. Using radio and few radio-discussion talk shows, the production sold out over a week ago. In addition to this concert version, the producers are planning a fall road tour after the show has opened on Broadway (next Oct. at the Mark Hellinger Theatre).

Show employs arena staging now, and uses the best in lighting and sound. Performers move in and out of stage centre to add a new dimension to the best-selling Decca album. Everyone in the speaking cast of 30 plays their parts well. There were four standing ovations with strongest mitting for Yvonne Elliman, who repeated the Mary Magdalene part she sang on the album. Carl Anderson as Judas, Jeff Fenholt as Jesus and Alan Martin as King Herod are also standouts.

The evangelical fervour that greeted every number has religious connotation, but "Jesus Christ—Superstar" is entertainment for all. It should be very big on Broadway, putting "The Greatest Story Ever Told" to a rock beat.

'VARIETY'

He is portrayed as a rather....um....vague figure which people can't really identify with. They think, well this guy wasn't real. He....He couldn't've just gone around clutching sheep with a halo, I mean, but Christ obviously was, first and foremost, whether you believe He's God or not,

Feeding of the Five Thousand.

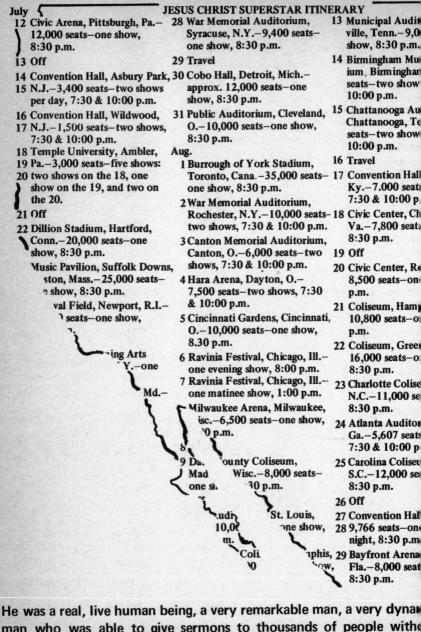

July | **JESUS CHRIST SUPERSTAR ITINERARY**

12 Civic Arena, Pittsburgh, Pa.—
12,000 seats—one show,
8:30 p.m.

13 Off

14 Convention Hall, Asbury Park,
15 N.J.—3,400 seats—two shows
per day, 7:30 & 10:00 p.m.

16 Convention Hall, Wildwood,
17 N.J.—1,500 seats—two shows,
7:30 & 10:00 p.m.

18 Temple University, Ambler,
19 Pa.—3,000 seats—five shows:
20 two shows on the 18, one
show on the 19, and two on
the 20.

21 Off

22 Dillion Stadium, Hartford,
Conn.—20,000 seats—one
show, 8:30 p.m.

Music Pavilion, Suffolk Downs,
ston, Mass.—25,000 seats—
e show, 8:30 p.m.

val Field, Newport, R.I.—
seats—one show,

ing Arts
Y.—one

Md.—

28 War Memorial Auditorium,
Syracuse, N.Y.—9,400 seats—
one show, 8:30 p.m.

29 Travel

30 Cobo Hall, Detroit, Mich.—
approx. 12,000 seats—one
show, 8:30 p.m.

31 Public Auditorium, Cleveland,
O.—10,000 seats—one show,
8:30 p.m.

Aug.

1 Burrough of York Stadium,
Toronto, Cana.—35,000 seats—
one show, 8:30 p.m.

2 War Memorial Auditorium,
Rochester, N.Y.—10,000 seats—
two shows, 7:30 & 10:00 p.m.

3 Canton Memorial Auditorium,
Canton, O.—6,000 seats—two
shows, 7:30 & 10:00 p.m.

4 Hara Arena, Dayton, O.—
7,500 seats—two shows, 7:30
& 10:00 p.m.

5 Cincinnati Gardens, Cincinnati,
O.—10,000 seats—one show,
8.30 p.m.

6 Ravinia Festival, Chicago, Ill.—
one evening show, 8:00 p.m.

7 Ravinia Festival, Chicago, Ill.—
one matinee show, 1:00 p.m.

Milwaukee Arena, Milwaukee,
isc.—6,500 seats—one show,
0 p.m.

8

9 Da   ounty Coliseum,
Mad   Wisc.—8,000 seats—
one sh   30 p.m.

udi   St. Louis,
10,0   one show,
m.

Coli   phis,
0   ow,

13 Municipal Audit
ville, Tenn.—9,0
show, 8:30 p.m.

14 Birmingham Mu
ium, Birmingham
seats—two show
10:00 p.m.

15 Chattanooga Au
Chattanooga, Te
seats—two show
10:00 p.m.

16 Travel

17 Convention Hall
Ky.—7.000 seats
7:30 & 10:00 p

18 Civic Center, Ch
Va.—7,800 seats
8:30 p.m.

19 Off

20 Civic Center, R
8,500 seats—on
p.m.

21 Coliseum, Hamp
10,800 seats—o
p.m.

22 Coliseum, Gree
16,000 seats—o
8:30 p.m.

23 Charlotte Colise
N.C.—11,000 se
8:30 p.m.

24 Atlanta Auditor
Ga.—5,607 seats
7:30 & 10:00 p

25 Carolina Coliseu
S.C.—12,000 se
8:30 p.m.

26 Off

27 Convention Hall
28 9,766 seats—on
night, 8:30 p.m

29 Bayfront Arena
Fla.—8,000 seat
8:30 p.m.

He was a real, live human being, a very remarkable man, a very dyna
man who was able to give sermons to thousands of people witho
microphones. He was able to lose His temper and....and....and at
same time, be incredibly calm and serene as He was, you know, in

Christ Walks upon the Lake.

off
Municipal Aud
la.–12,00
:30 p.m.

Municipal Auditorium, N
Orleans, La.–7,000 seats–tw
shows, 7:30 & 10:00 p.m.
Hirsh Memorial Auditorium
Shroveport, La.–10,000 s
one show, 8:30 p.m.
Coliseum, Little Rock, Ar
0,000 seats–one show,
:30 p.m.
City Center, Tulsa, Okla.–
0,000 seats–one show,
:30 p.m.
Wichita State Field House,
Wichita, Kan.–8,500 seats–
one show, 8:30 p.m.
Municipal Auditorium, Kansas
City, Mo.–10,250 seats–one
how, 8:30 p.m.
off
Fairground Arena, Oklahoma
City, Okla.–10,000 seats–
one show, 8:30 p.m.
Tarrant County, Fort Worth,
Tex.–10,000 seats–one show,
:30 p.m.
Coliseum, Dallas, Tex.–
0,000 seats, one show,
:30 p.m.

13 m.
Ant
one
4 Off
15 Colise
10,0
8:30 p.m
16 Off
17 Coliseu   , Tex.–7,500
seats–o   ow, 8:30 p.m.
18 University Fieldhouse,
Albquerque, N. Mex.–10,000
seats, one show, 8:30 p.m.
19 Off
20 Coliseum, Phoenix, Arix.–
13,000 seats–one show
8:30 p.m.
21 Off
22 Orange County Swing
Auditorium, San Bernardino,
Calif.–8,000 seats–one show,
8:30 p.m.
23 Sports arena San Die
Calif.–8,000 seats–
8:30 p.m.
23 Sports Arena,
Calif.–12,00
show, 8:30 p.
H   wood Bo
18,000 s
day,
s Ange
one
.
resti
20,00

Houst
enn.–12,5 one s
8:30 p.m.
10 Houston Coliseum,
Tex.–12,000 seats
per night, 8:30 p.m
11 Civic Center, Balti
.12,000 seats–one
8:30 p.m.
12

mean can you dig it? We're like the circus. When people are having breakfast,
're moving into town. We're setting up lights when they're having lunch. When
ey're having supper we're rehearsing. Just so they can spend an hour and a half
th us. It's like the goddamn circus."

Road Manager Concert Tour Two

y last hours and um....um....I sort of found that Christ the man
ant much more to me when I sort of read in between the lines, um....
the uh....FROST: What about....what about people who say about
stage production really that Judas is the star more than Jesus. Now,

Controversy on the Tradition of the Elders.

PURCHASERS OF
JESUS CHRIST, SUPERSTAR TICKETS
(BEWARE!)

PERHAPS YOU ARE UNAWARE THAT THERE IS ONLY ONE TOURING COMPANY OF JESUS CHRIST SUPERSTAR THAT HAS BEEN AUTHORIZED BY THE WRITERS, ANDREW LLOYD WEBER AND TIM RICE. THERE ARE OTHER COMPANIES WHICH USE THE NAME BUT ARE NOT AUTHORIZED TO PERFORM THE ALBUM IN ITS ENTIRETY. THERE ARE DIFFERENCES WHICH YOU, AS THE BUYING PUBLIC, SHOULD BE MADE AWARE OF BEFORE PURCHASING A TICKET.

1) Unauthorized companies (unauthorized by the Robert Stigwood company which owns the rights to the complete staging and album recording of Superstar) are not able to perform the opera in its entirety.

2) Other companies do not have an orchestra of 32 people, a chorus of 17, a rock band of 7 and three leads. Other companies carry a considerably smaller cast.

3) Other companies do not carry as complete a sound system and professional lighting personnel so that you are not able to enjoy this fantastic show as conceived by the authors.

4) The authorized company has performed in major cities such as Detroit, Cleveland, Pittsburgh, and Chicago, where critics have given the show rave reviews.

REMEMBER: The original authorized show is being performed in Minneapolis October 19, Metropolitan Sports Center. We guarantee you the finest performance of Superstar as originally recorded. Don't be fooled by other companies.

Tickets to the real performance: $4.50, 5.50, & 6.50.
Mail order: Greathall, 1624 Harmon Pl., Mpls.
Please enclose a stamped self-addressed envelope.
Phone for info: 332-6666 or 333-1201
—Robert Stigwood Organization

I mean, I didn't find that with the record, but I....but Judas is a m colourful sort of a fellow....ANDREW: I think, one thing....FROST: the stage. ANDREW: I would say that I think if this is our fault, I th that Jesus is not so well written, certainly from my fault rea

The Syro-Phœnician Woman.

sically, I don't think, as Judas and um....I....FROST: You mean, it's
-write of the old....Judas has got all the best tunes like....ANDREW:
no, not really....ANDREW: No, I don't think that....ANDREW:
ause I think Jesus actually has the....I mean, 'Gethsemane', to me, is

The Second Miracle of Feeding.

the....is the high point of the whole thing, I mean, to me the last v
of 'Gethsemane' is the....is musically the whole high point of the dra
but it's just that I think that, you know, it often happens when yo
writing something, I think, your central dramatic figure, if you're s

The Deaf and Dumb Man in Decapolis.

ANNAS
With no crowd around him

CAIAPHAS
Then we can't fail

BLOOD MONEY

JUDAS

I don't need your blood money!

CAIAPHAS
Oh that doesn't matter our expenses are good

JUDAS
I don't want your blood money!

ANNAS
But you might as well take it—we think that you should

CAIAPHAS
Think of the things you can do with that money
Choose any charity—give to the poor
We've noted your motives—we've noted your feelings
This isn't blood money—it's a fee nothing
Fee nothing, fee nothing more.

JUDAS
On Thursday night you'll find him where you want him
Far from the crowds in the Garden of Gethsemane

CHOIR
Well done Judas
Good old Judas

and beginning, is not necessarily the thing you cope with best, but
re going to try and....FROST: But I think, yes....I mean, I think
t's a very modest answer, but I would have thought that in practice...
1: We also see Judas....FROST: The difference between the stage and

Warning against the Leaven of the Pharisees.

THE LAST SUPPER
Thursday night, The Last Supper

APOSTLES

Look at all my trials and tribulations
   Sinking in a gentle pool of wine
   Don't disturb me now I can see the answers
Till this evening is this morning life is fine
Always hoped that I'd be an apostle
Knew that I would make it if I tried
Then when we retire we can write the gospels
So they'll still talk about us when we've died

JESUS

The end...
Is just a little harder when brought about by friends
For all you care this wine could be my blood
For all you care this bread could be my body
The end!
This is my blood you drink
This is my body you eat
If you would remember me when you eat and drink...
I must be mad thinking I'll be remembered—yes
I must be out of my head!
Look at your blank faces! My name will mean nothing
Ten minutes after I'm dead!
One of you denies me
One of you betrays me—

APOSTLES

Not I! Who would? Impossible!

the record, because I don't think the criticism applies on the reco
TIM: Possibly, um....also we are seeing Judas, in a way, in a dual r
we are trying to make him Everyman and I think one of the interest
things about the tragedy of Judas and his life obviously, you know, v

A Blind Man Healed at Bethsaida.

e Robert Stigwood Group Ltd. of London and William Morris Agency are
termined to enforce their "Jesus Christ, Superstar" interests in the courts,
ardless of legal decisions in the case. They have been seeking injunctions
inst "unauthorized" performances.

ter Brown, Stigwood president, cited a victory in Federal Court, New York,
inst Canadian Rock Opera Co.'s show scheduled for the International Hotel
Las Vegas.

said a ruling recently by U.S. Court of Appeals for the 2nd Circuit is mislead-
, that it is actually a denial rather than an approval. The court held that the
nce granted to American Program Bureau by ASCAP, for performances of
sical selections from the opera, is authorized as long as the separate songs are
livered without costumes, scenery, pantomime or dancing.

hat is correct," Brown said, "but it also says they cannot advertise 'Jesus
rist, Superstar' in any way, shape or manner. Anybody can sing songs from
opera but they cannot mention its name . . ."

st month Stigwood had sought a temporary restraining order against Superstar,
Missouri company, in Washington, D.C.'s Constitution Hall.

the civil action filed in U.S. District Court for the District of Columbia,
fendant's counsel contended that "Jesus Christ Superstar, a Rock Opera"
s not in reality an opera, but was rather an album set. This was in reference
the performance scheduled for Constitution Hall, which was halted. Defence
imed the works were "merely a collection of ordinary musical compositions
ilable for public performance."

CAP. Counsel contended that Superstar Productions Ltd., was a licensee of
nerican Society of Composers, Authors & Publishers, hence was "licenced to
g, stage, or perform any and all musical compositions contained in the current
alogue of the said ASCAP."

perstar counsel's counterclaim sought damages of $1 million from plaintiffs
halting the Washington engagements, plus $9,807 for expenses and costs
urred in preparation for staging the performance, plus $20,995.50 in deprived
eipts.

previously announced, however, MCA Inc. of Universal City, Calif., and the
igwood Organization of London had agreed to adapt the album by Andrew
oyd Webber and Tim Rice into a New York stage production, and a concurrent
ming of that property into a motion picture for Universal.

uperstar" will also be co-produced by the two companies as a concert attrac-
n, with two groups touring for one year, having started July 14 at Convention
ll in Asbury Park. The second will start in the fall for college audiences.

**isaster to put it mildly, um....FROST: Yes. TIM: Basically, the
son why things went so badly for him wasn't because he was um....
ically evil, but because he was very intelligent and he was a super
ctical man and this is the appeal of the story that you have Judas**

St. Peter's great Declaration of Belief.

United States Court of Appeals
FOR THE SECOND CIRCUIT

Docket No. 71-2057

The Robert Stigwood Group Limited, Leeds Music Limited and Leeds Music Corporation,
Plaintiffs-Cross-Appellants,

against

Betty Sperber, individually and doing business as The Original American Touring Company and Betty Sperber Management, Inc.,
Defendants-Appellants.

INTERLOCUTORY APPEAL FROM THE UNITED STATES DISTRICT COURT FOR THE SOUTHERN DISTRICT OF NEW YORK

The Robert Stigwood Group, Rice, Timothy, et al.	American Program Bureau, et al. vs. (Southern District New York)
The Robert Stigwood Group Limited, et al.	America Rock Opera Company, et al. vs. Hawaii (United States District Court For The District of Hawaii)
The Robert Stigwood Group Limited, et al.	Aquarius Theatre, et al. vs. (United States District Court Central District of California)
The Robert Stigwood Group Limited, MCA Canada Ltd., et al.	Bendell, John d/b/a National Rock Opera Company vs. (Federal Court of Canada Trial Division)
The Robert Stigwood Group Limited, et al.	City and County of Denver, a vs. municipal corporation (United States District Court For The District of Colorado)
The Robert Stigwood Group Limited, et al.	Kenny Gordon, et ano. vs. (United States District Court Grand Rapids, Western Division Michigan)
The Robert Stigwood Group Limited, et al.	Hilton Hotels Corporation, et al. vs. (United States District Court Southern District of New York)
The Robert Stigwood Group Limited, et al.	Lon Hurwitz, et al. vs. (United States District Court Southern District of New York)
The Robert Stigwood Group Limited, et al.	Jesus Christ Superstar, et al. vs. (Toledo, Ohio) United States District Court Northern District of Ohio Western Division

the....the all-time practical man who wants to know what's going happen right now, you know, the Romans are going to clobber us everything, and the clash between Christ, the super spiritual man, in a sort of strange way they were both right, I mean, um, this isn'

First Prediction of the Passion.

The Robert Stigwood Group Limited, et al.	William Ashwood Kavanna, et al. vs. (Southern District New York)
The Robert Stigwood Group Limited, et al.	Kenneth Lipsitz vs. United States District Court Milwaukee
The Robert Stigwood Group Limited, et al.	Milwaukee County War Memorial vs. Center, Inc., et al. (United States District Court Milwaukee)
The Robert Stigwood Group Limited, et al.	Superstar Productions, Ltd., vs. Milwaukee Auditorium Board and Fred Muth (United States District Court Milwaukee)
The Robert Stigwood Group Limited, et al.	Mid-America Rock Organization, vs. Inc., et al. (Southern District of Illinois Northern Division)
The Robert Stigwood Group Limited, et al.	Miami Hollywood Sportatorium, vs. Inc., et al. (United States District Court Southern District of Florida)
The Robert Stigwood Group Limited, et al.	Miami Hai-Alai, Inc., et al. vs. (United States District Court Southern District of Florida)
The Robert Stigwood Group Limited, et al.	Music Productions, et al. vs. (United States District Court Orlando Division)
The Robert Stigwood Group Limited, et al.	Russell Patterson, et al. vs. (United States District Court Western District of Missouri Western Division)
The Robert Stigwood Group Limited, et al.	Repertory Theatre of America, vs. Inc., et al. (United States District Court Southern District of Ohio Eastern Division)
The Robert Stigwood Group Limited, et al.	Pierre Robin vs. Repertory Theatre of America (United States District Court District of Columbus, Ohio)
The Robert Stigwood Group Limited, et al.	Barry E. Singer, Frontier Talent vs. Corporation, Don Calvert and Norman Marzano (United States District Court New Jersey)
The Robert Stigwood Group Limited, et al.	Betty Sperber, et ano. vs. (Southern District New York)
The Robert Stigwood Group Limited, et al.	Superstar Productions, Ltd., vs. et al. (Washington, D.C.)

…bert Stigwood, Chairman of the Robert Stigwood Group, released …day the figures for the first month's gross for his organization's …ficial road company production of "Jesus Christ—Superstar." The …mpany which opened in Pittsburgh on July 12, grossed $1,300,000 …the first 4 weeks of its engagements, representing dates in 19 cities.

…though the road company was originally scheduled for a limited …nonth run, Stigwood has since amended the original plan and will …ep the first company on the road for a full year. He estimates the …ar's gross will be in excess of $12,000,000.

…gest at all that Judas is on a par with Christ, I mean, this isn't what …suggesting, but one can see the logic of Judas' argument and....and...
it was absolutely inevitable that they would clash and I cannot …eve that Judas was just a tool of God's will that somebody created

The Transfiguration.

SYDNEY—

A leading Australian entrepreneur and a group of Sydney nuns were locked today in a legal battle over rights to production of the hit rock musical "Jesus Christ, Superstar".

Sisters from Loreto Convent said they received permission from Leeds Music, which holds the world music copyright, to perform the musical at their conven

Entrepreneur Harry Miller threatened an injunction to prohibit the nuns from staging the show.

Miller is Australian representative for the British company Robert Stigwood which holds the world copyright for the play.

Miller, who plans to stage the rock opera in Adelaide next March, said Leeds Music could not have given the nuns permission to stage the play even if the company had wanted to because it only holds copyright to the musical score, not the performance of the play.

The nuns, who intend to put on the performance in two weeks, were not available for comment.

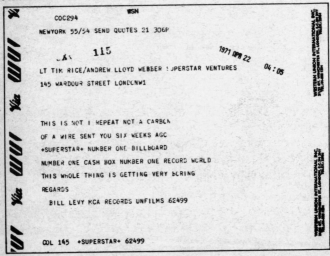

```
WSN
COC294
NEWYORK 55/54 SEND QUOTES 21 306P

    .A:   115                          1971 APR 22
LT TIM RICE/ANDREW LLOYD WEBBER SUPERSTAR VENTURES   04:05
145 WARDOUR STREET LONDONW1


THIS IS NOT I REPEAT NOT A CARBON
OF A WIRE SENT YOU SIX WEEKS AGO
+SUPERSTAR+ NUMBER ONE BILLBOARD
NUMBER ONE CASH BOX NUMBER ONE RECORD WORLD
THIS WHOLE THING IS GETTING VERY BORING
REGARDS
    BILL LEVY MCA RECORDS UNFILMS 62499

COL 145  +SUPERSTAR+ 62499
```

purely to be evil, I'm not trying to exonerate him in the lyrics, but just saying that anybody could have been in that position. ANDREW don't think, for me, Judas is a particularly sympathetic personalit mean, musically, he's not sort of....TIM: He's a very weak characte

Healing of the Lunatic Boy.

LIFE

Worldwide Success of 'Jesus Christ Superstar'

A REVERENT ROCK OPERA

Chris Brown
in the role
of Christ

MAY 28 • 1971 • 50¢

DREW: He seems to be a bit weak and one might say, well, I mean,
....I....I....I would like to feel that one should have compassion about
ybody, I want you to say, well one can understand his point of
, I mean, he must have had a case, otherwise he wouldn't have done

Thou art the Christ, the Son of the living God.

JESUS CHRIST, Superstar, has now become the most rewarding record ever produced in the U.K. Its world sales are valued at over £13m., pushing it ahead of the Beatle's *Sergeant Pepper.* And this has been achieved in just over a year. No wonder a grateful Minister at the Board of Trade this month personally presented gold discs to the two young composers, Andrew Lloyd Webber and Tim Rice. What's more, there is still money to be made. Demand from the U.K. has been slack and only 40,000 sets of the LP have so far been sold. When the stage show—and eventually the film—arrive, the record should really take off. In the U.S., for example, £10m. has been spent on the music.

it, he must have felt something, he must....he must have had some k
of human thoughts and emotions. FROST: Well, let's move on t
later part now in Jesus Christ Super Star and welcome Barry Denn
who plays the part of Pontius Pilate....we welcome Barry Denne

And upon this rock I will build my church

"Listen, the concerts are making $70,000 a week, the records have grossed 35 million, and we've just said hello."

Ned Tannen
Head of Production
Universal Pictures.

Universal City, Calif.—Lew R. Wasserman, President of MCA, Inc., announced that the company's earnings for the first half of 1971 were 18% higher than those for the first six months of 1970.

Wasserman added that over two million double record albums and tapes of the rock opera "Jesus Christ Superstar" have been sold and this has contributed important-antly to the historically high revenues of the record and music publishing divisions.

"It's not a record, it's an industry."
Lew Wasserman

pping)....Come and sit down for a moment before you....DENNEN: nk you. FROST: Before you work for us, which we look forward to a second or two very much. This must be....how many different ws....you've done so many different shows before this one, this

And the gates of Hades shall not prevail against it.

" 'Jesus Christ Superstar' has already grossed thirty million dollars. Just where did we go wrong?"

"I remember when the boys first came over several of my colleagues at the seminary said to me "If I was the bishop I'd hire them at $10,000 apiece to write several more stories from the scriptures because they certainly speak to the times."

Father Harold Buckley
New York Seminarien

must be very different to anything else you've ever done, is it? DENNI
I've never done an opera. FROST: Right—and this is a modern op
DENNEN: This is an opera and I've never done rock really, at all,
stuck with musical comedy mostly. FROST: What about the things

I will give unto thee the keys of the kingdom of heaven.

JESUS
Peter will deny me in just a few hours
Three times will deny me—and that's not all I see
One of you here dining, one of my twelve chosen
Will leave to betray me—

JUDAS
Cut out the dramatics! You know very well who—

JESUS
Why don't you go do it?

JUDAS
You want me to do it!

JESUS
Hurry they are waiting

JUDAS
If you knew why I do it...

JESUS
I don't care why you do it!

JUDAS
To think I admired you
For now I despise you

JESUS
You liar—you Judas

JUDAS
You want me to do it!
What if I just stayed here
And ruined your ambition?
Christ you deserve it!

...re talking about with Yvonne just now, do you find audiences, do
...find people, respond differently to Jesus Christ Super Star than
...ther hit show? DENNEN: Yeah, we get a lot of freaky people, there
...a lot....there are a lot of young kids who come back stage too and....

First Prediction of the Passion.

JESUS

Hurry you fool, hurry and go,
Save me your speeches, I don't want to know—Go!

APOSTLES

Look at all my trials and tribulations
Sinking in a gentle pool of wine
What's that in the bread it's gone to my head
Till this morning is this evening life is fine
Always hoped that I'd be an apostle
Knew that I would make it if I tried
Then when we retire we can write the gospels
So they'll all talk about us when we've died

JUDAS

You sad pathetic man—see where you've brought us to
Our ideals die around us all because of you
And now the saddest cut of all—
Someone has to turn you in
Like a common criminal, like a wounded animal
A jaded mandarin
A jaded mandarin
A jaded faded mandarin

JESUS

Get out! They're waiting! They're waiting for you!

JUDAS

Everytime I look at you I don't understand
Why you let the things you did get so out of hand
You'd have managed better if you'd had it planned—

APOSTLES

Look at all my trials and tribulations
Sinking in a gentle pool of wine

it's always been my dream to be ripped apart by young people
(laughter)....the first few times I ostentatiously went out of the exe
tive offices door, you know, and I thought well I'll try it and I went
the stage door and....(laughter)....they didn't want to know. FROS

The Transfiguration.

The Broadway production of
esus Christ, Superstar" is
pected to have nearly
,400,000 in advance sales
fore the preem Tuesday at
rk Hellinger theatre. It is a
bert Stigwood-MCA pro-
ction, being mounted by
m O'Horgan.

"I
like
to fill
the stage
with lots of
things to look at"
Tom O'Horgan

e been thinking about *Superstar* since
vember '70," says Tom, director of
, *Lenny*, the just-about-opening on
adway musical, *Inner City*. O'Horgan
d many approaches to *Superstar*,
lly realized the opera through "a mystic
d of Blake area by way of Peter Max,
gritte . . . It's another kind of revelation
ne—an exaltation. Theatre and religion
e always celebrated some kind of
tyr—Dionysius, Christ, Lenny Bruce.
interpretation of religion is to intensify
f your life impulses. Theatre is my
ression of religion. *Hair* or *Futz* are
ply religious plays . . . *Superstar's*
ly about: nobody's perfect. That's
t it's about . . . leading if fully and
g turned on. The only sin I recognize
onfulfillment of the life urge."

y didn't....they're just not interested in Pontius Pilate....how
resting....that's very interesting....so it is very different from....
NEN: And we get strange letters occasionally....(laughter)....I've
r gotten one, but the cast itself has gotten some really peculiar

Healing of the Lunatic Boy.

MARK HELLINGER THEATRE

Robert Stigwood
in association with MCA, Inc.
By arrangement with David Land

presents

JESUS CHRIST SUPERSTAR

Lyrics by **TIM RICE** *Music by* **ANDREW LLOYD WEBBER**

with

**JEFF FENHOLT YVONNE ELLIMAN BEN VEREEN CARL ANDERSON
SETH ALLEN PAUL AINSLEY STEPHEN KLEIN
RANDALL'S ISLAND**

Associate Producers
GATCHELL AND NEUFELD

| *Scenic design by* | *Lighting designed by* | *Costumes designed by* | *Sound designed by* |
| **ROBIN WAGNER** | **JULES FISHER** | **RANDY BARCELO** | **ABE JACOB** |

| *Musical direction by* | *Orchestrations by* | *Production Supervisor* |
| **MARC PRESSEL** | **ANDREW LLOYD WEBBER** | **CHARLES GRAY** |

Conceived for the stage and directed by
TOM O'HORGAN

Original Broadway Cast Album On

9

letters which have been put on the bulletin board, um....people pray
for us and our souls....(laughter)....telling us which hotel they we
staying at that week....it's....FROST: People praying for you all ov
the country....ought to be a good feeling. What's the....the....which

The Temple Tribute.

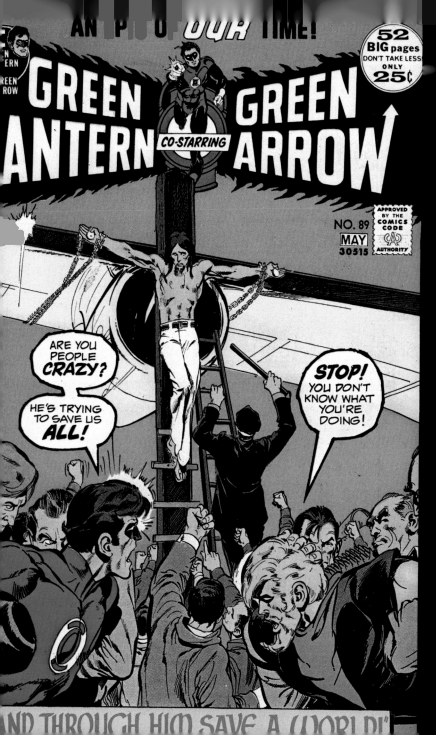

"JESUS CHRIST SUPERSTAR"— Jeff Fenholt, as Christ, is borne aloft by His followers in the musical work that depicts His last seven days on earth. Staged by Tom O'Horgan, the production features Yvonne Elliman as Mary Magdalene and Ben Vereen as Judas Iscariot. Tuesday at the Mark Hellinger.

*he title page of the program
"Jesus Christ Superstar" at
Mark Hellinger stresses that
m O'Horgan has not only
ected the production but has
nceived" it. It is not an
maculate conception."*
    *—Walter Kerr
      The New York Times*

*e entire production looks
her like a Radio City Music
ll show into whose producers'
l designers' coffee cups the
er had slipped some LSD."*
    *—John Simon
      New York Magazine*

by RAUSCH

"I don't read reviews very much."
    —Tom O'Horgan

t....tell us about the number you're going to do now for us.
NNEN: Well, this is Pilate's dream, which is very early on in the
w and, of course, Bible readers everywhere know that Pilate never
ly did have a dream, it was his wife who had the dream, as my wife

The Apostles' Ambition rebuked.

heater: Christ's Passion Transported to the Stage in Guise of Serious

'Jesus Christ Superstar' Billed as Rock Opera

By CLIVE BARNES

Nothing could convince me that any show that has sold two-and-one-half million copies of its album before the opening night is anything like all bad. But I must also confess to experiencing some disappointment when "Jesus Christ Superstar" opened at the Mark Hellinger Theater last night.

It all rather resembled one's first sight of the Empire State Building. Not at all uninteresting, but somewhat unsurprising and of minimal artistic value.

Not for the first time has Jesus Christ been made big business. This musical—already very successful on records—tells the story of the Passion of Christ in contemporary terms and accompanied by pop music, ranging from rock-salt to icing-sugar. The story will doubtless be familiar to most. The lyrics are by Tim Rice and the music by Andrew Lloyd Webber. They are young Englishmen of obvious talent, and it is apparent that this midcult version of the Passion story is seriously and sincerely intended.

Mr. Rice's intention was clearly to place Christ's betrayal and death into a

Jeff Fenholt in the title role

vernacular more immediate perhaps to our times. His record sales would presumably indicate his success in this aim, but he does not have a very happy ear for the

The Cast

JESUS CHRIST SUPERSTAR, a rock opera. Lyrics by Tim Rice, music by Andrew Lloyd Webber; settings by Robin Wagner; lighting by Jules Fisher; costumes by Randy Barcelo; sound designed by Taplin Productions; musical direction by Marc Pressel; orchestrations by Andrew Lloyd Webber; conceived and directed by Tom O'Horgan; production supervisor, Charles Gray. Presented by Robert Stigwood, in association with MCA, Inc., by arrangement with David Land; Gatchell and Neufeld, associate producers. At the Mark Hellinger Theater, 51st Street west of Broadway.

Judas Iscariot .... Ben Vereen
Jesus of Nazareth ...... Jeff Fenholt
Mary Magdalene ...... Yvonne Elliman

English language. There is a certain air of dogged doggerel about his phrases that too often sound as limp as a deflated priest.

It is surely unfortunate,

even bathetic, to have Christ at his moment of death remark solemnly: "God forgive them? They don't know what they are doing." The sentiments are unassailable, but the language is unforgivably pedestrian. Again — in another lyric — we have Christ complaining bitterly:

"My time is about through —little left to do—After all I've tried for three years . . . seems like 30 . . . seems like 30."

Well, of course, it sounds better set to music, but not, I feel, better enough.

The music itself is extraordinarily eclectic. It runs so many gamuts it almost becomes a musical cartel. Mr. Lloyd Webber is an accomplished musician—he is one of those rare birds, a Broadway composer who produces his own orchestrations—and he has emerged with some engaging numbers.

The title song, "Superstar," has a bounce and

exaltation to it, an almost revivalist fervor that deserves its popularity. I also much admire the other hit of the show, "I Don't Know How to Love Him." This also shows Mr. Rice at his best as a lyricist, although it is perhaps surprising to find this torch ballad sung by Mary Magdalene to Jesus Christ—even a Jesus Christ Superstar. There is a certain vulgarity here typical of an age that takes a peculiar delight in painting mustaches on the "Mona Lisa" and demonstrating that every great man was a regular guy at heart.

Most of the music is pleasant, although unmemorable. It has a pleasing texture, although the orchestral finale, which "sounds something like a church-organ voluntary inspired by Vaughan Williams and Massenet may be a little hard to take for musical ears. The pastiches of the Beatles are far more acceptable, but this is not an important rock score in the manner of "Tommy" by The Who. It is, unhappily, neither innovative nor original.

The music does have the bustling spirit of vitality, which is what has made its records sell, and what Tom O'Horgan has seized upon in his monumentally ingenious staging. Ever since his beginning at La Mama, Mr. O'Horgan has tried to startle us. Once he startled us with small things, now he startles us with big things. This time, the things got too big.

There were too many purely decorative effects, artistic excrescences dreamed up by the director and his designers, Robin Wagner and Randy Barcelo, that seemed intended to make us gasp and our blood run cold. The stage is full of platforms, carriages descend from the heavens, and even the stars over Gethsemene are captured in a blue plastic box. The total effect is brilliant but cheap—like

Music's Vitali to O'Horgan

the Christmas dec a chic Fifth Aven

●

It is unfortunate sound equipment sounded rather b cidentially—involv of hand-mikes, w dressed up as piec and occasionally round from acto like holy chalices, unmistakably mi least when Jesus dramatically to se the approved TV a manner.

For me, the real d ment came not in —which is better of-the-mill Broadw best score for a musical in years— conception. There ness in its contem a sneaky pleasur boldness of its ima a special, undefine smugness in its Christ is updated, b I felt, renewed

●

The performance second fiddle to the of the record album virtuosity of Mr. C own performance. C made into a shr neurotic, who look the right pictures, plaved with some Jeff Fenholt. But h a rewarding view although at one limp-wristed, rosil laged Herod, the conniving Caiapha spitefully Roman Pr last was a good pe by Barry Denen, mired the tortured Ben Vereen, an sung Marv Mag Yvonne Elliman—o few survivors f album.

For all this, " seemed to me less t —but the novelty o rations should win adherents.

"But whoever shall smite thee on thy right cheek, turn to him the other also"

pointed out to me during the casting, but we put it in really. FRO Have Women's Lib complained about your taking away the d (laughter)....ANDREW: Very good point....TIM: As a matter of fa FROST: Why did you do it, you pigs, why did you do it? DENN

Discipline in the Church.

A Supershow Called 'Jesus Christ Superstar' Arrives

By DOUGLAS WATT

"Jesus Christ Superstar," which as everybody knows opened last night at the linger, is so stunningly effective a theatrical experience that I am still finding it icult to compose my thoughts about it. It is, in short, a triumph.

is is, of course, the ultimate zation of a work that had to prove itself by means of cording that has been a best-r for a year. The recording s the impression of a dra-c oratorio with no real hint ow it might play on a stage.

Tom O'Horgan, who con-ed the production and direct-c, has brought the work to ant life. It's by far the best g he has ever done.

A Fine Score

s I'm sure you know, "Jesus st Superstar," which tells its y entirely through song, con-rs the seven last days of st in contemporary pop terms it must be added, with com-e reverence.

ndrew Lloyd Webber's score ibrant, richly varied and al-s dramatically right and n the same things can be said Tim Rice's lyrics.

e songs are, indeed, marvel-and although they rock a good of the time there are other esting influences in it—y handled references to Pro-ev and Weill, to name two, some lovely string and al writing.

arting with what is basically re, raked stage, O'Horgan has it ablaze with action (it is ably the most energetic show ever seen) and special ef-s. I assume he worked closely scenic designer Robin Wag-lighting designer Jules Fish-nd costumer Randy Barcelo.

any case, by use of a daz-g assortment of set pieces t of them descending from flies), props · and costumes has filled the stage with and movement.

r examples: Caiaphas and as drift down and hover

Jeff Fenholt
Sings title role

over the scene below on a kind of elaborate bower; Judas, a rope round his neck, is hauled, first twitching and then limp, up out of sight; a monstrous green head opens to reveal King Herod reclining in a pink shell; and so on.

Splendid Cast

But the score and the per-formance of a marvelous cast are what count most. I suppose you'd have to call Judas the star role since it is psychologically the most arresting one, and here a baritone named Ben Vereen is simply magnificent, singing and acting with a vitality that is almost unbelievable and yet with nuance, as well.

Jeff Fenholt, in the title role is also well cast, pale and slender

and with a tenor voice that can croon or scream to startling ef-fect. His "Gethsemane" was beautifully done.

Yvonne Elliman, the only mem-ber of the cast heard on the re-cording, was a sweet-voiced Mary Magdalene whose "I Don't Know How to Love Him" was exquisite-ly sung.

Paul Ainsley's Herod is a heav-ily-rouged man on absurdly high platform footwear and he stop-ped the show with his Charles-ton, "King Herod's Song." Barry Dennen was a chilling figure, in-deed, as Pontius Pilate, and Bob Bingham as Caiaphas and Phil Jethro as Annas were also first-rate.

But so is the entire cast, whose movements O'Horgan has choreo-graphed with such skill.

I must say a word, too, about the elaborate sound arrangements which has the leading performers working with gray-padded hand mikes and the pit orchestra, un-der Marc Pressel, divided, some by glass, into sections. It worked so well that all the words sung by the unusually articulate princi-pals came through clearly.

The story in itself is, of course, almost unbearably moving, but the great accomplishment of Webber and Rice has been to make it so strikingly immediate.

, I needed a number in the first act....FROST: Oh, I see, (laughter)
: We wanted to have a dream sequence which would have some-g in the first half of the opera which sort of foretold the second and in....basically, it was going to be Calpurnia, Pilate's wife, and

Duty of Forgiveness.

"Now we have him!" Jesus is arrested

we were still casting and then Barry turned up and was excellen
Pilate, so we thought, well, you know, he's good, so let's give Barr
dream....he's obviously the dreamer, I mean, there's obviously dou
to, if ever the dream existed at all, but and um....so we thought,

Parable of the Unforgiving Servant.

can have the dream, sing this song and we altered the lyrics
y, you know, and in fact, for the stage because Barry was also in
age and he was so good, we extended Pilate's bit even further so
rial sequences at the end are about twice the length they are on

Rejection of Christ by a Samaritan Village.

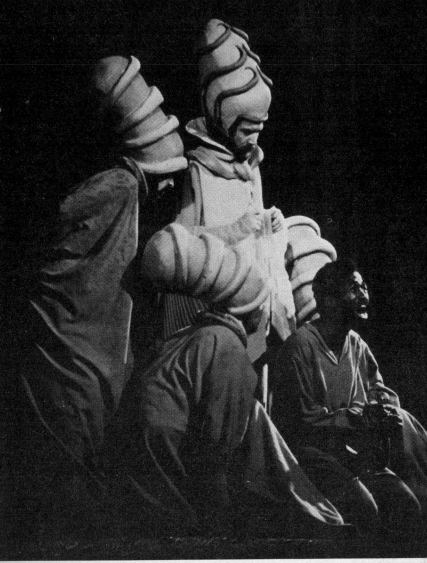

"Its a fee nothing more." Judas' betrayal

the record which is really, um....to get over the drama of Pilate vs. priests vs. the crowd vs. Pilate, you know, and um....also to give Barr bit more space. FROST: Well, we'd love to hear 'Pilate's Dream, Barr lovely...Barry Dennen—'Pilate's Dream'...(clapping)....FROST: Welco

Healing of the Blind Man at Jerusalem.

Don't disturb me now I can see the answers
Till this evening is this morning life is fine
Always hoped that I'd be an apostle
Knew that I would make it if I tried
Then when we retire we can write the gospels
So they'll still talk about us when we've died

SUS
Will no-one stay awake with me?
Peter? John? James?
Will none of you wait with me?
Peter? John? James?

GETHSEMANE
(I only want to say)
In the Garden of Gethsemane

SUS

I only want to say
If there is a way
Take this cup away from me for I don't want
to taste its poison
Feel it burn me, I have changed I'm not as sure
As when we started
Then I was inspired
Now I'm sad and tired
Listen surely I've exceeded expectations
Tried for three years seems like thirty
Could you ask as much from any other man?
But if I die
See the saga through and do the things you ask of me
Let them hate me hit me hurt me nail me to their tree
I'd wanna know I'd wanna know my God
I'd wanna see I'd wanna see my God
Why I should die

k on the subject of Jesus Christ Super Star. Thanks to Barry, that
marvellous, thank you very much indeed Barry for that number....
pping)....the....(clapping)....and now we've strolled over, as you can
to the piano, while Barry and Yvonne sit back and watch, in fact, we

Mission of the Seventy.

Would I be more noticed than I was ever before?
Would the things I've said and done matter any more?
I'd have to know I'd have to know my Lord
I'd have to see I'd have to see my Lord
If I die what will be my reward?
I'd have to know I'd have to know my Lord
Why should I die?
Can you show me now that I would not be killed in vain?
Show me just a little of your omnipresent brain
Show me there's a reason for your wanting me to die
You're far too keen on where and how and
    not so hot on why
Alright I'll die!
Just watch me die!
See how I die!
Then I was inspired
Now I'm sad and tired
After all I've tried for three years seems like ninety
Why then am I scared to finish what I started
What you started—I didn't start it
God thy will is hard
But you hold every card
I will drink your cup of poison, nail me to the cross
    and break me
Bleed me beat me kill me take me now—
    before I change my mind

THE ARREST

JUDAS

There he is! They're all asleep—the fools!

all sit back and watch because we wanted to say now....you're at
piano, now how did you operate in this, how many songs did
reject, for instance from Jesus Christ Super Star, how many songs
you alter, how did you go about that? ANDREW: Well, I can't rem

Parable of the Good Samaritan.

*ome—An enthusiastic endorsement of "Jesus Christ Superstar" was
*ven by the Rev. Billy Graham at a press conference here with the
*atement that "it will probably be the most successful Broadway
*how of all time." Earlier, Graham had criticized the rock opera for
iling to emphasize the divinity of Christ.

*a citing the play's success, Graham quoted Mao as saying that a
*evolution is something which must not only call for belief, but it
*ust be experienced. The same, he said, is the case with "Jesus Christ
uperstar."

"Jesus in a Broadway rock musical—how can Billy Graham compete with that!"

how many we rejected, he....we had....we had two or three that
*retly we were getting very unhappy with, there was one thing which
*s using the same tune as 'Heaven on their mind' where we were
ling with the fig tree where Jesus cursed the fig tree in the Bible, but

"I remember the first time I spoke to David Land he said it could go on forever
Can't you see the complete Old and New Testaments in cassettes? The
possibilities are endless."

Father Harold Buck

we....we just didn't think it worked very well and there wasn't sort
wasn't sort of very well....wasn't one of our better ones. FROST: W
about, for instance, the song, one of the songs that's caused....did
King Herod song, which the way it was staged and so on has cau

Martha.

SUPERSTAR AT BLOOMINGDALE'S

The Archbishop of Canterbury said in New York yesterday that the Broadway musical "Jesus Christ Superstar" contained "dreadful crudities" of presentation. Although some of the lyrics were very haunting, the show seemed to reject Christ's deity "from first to last". But, he said "something near to Christianity occasionally leaps out."

Jeff Fenholt, star of "Jesus Christ Superstar," will be at Bloomingdale's Friday, March 17th. Come chat with Jeff from 2:00 to 4:00 P.M. He'll be autographing copies of his original Broadway cast recording, "Jesus Christ Superstar," on albums, tapes and cartridges, in our new Radio/Television Department, 6th Floor, New York only.

Bloomingdale's, Lexington at 59th Street, New York, N.Y. 10022 · EL 5-5900

t controversy and so in New York but was that a first time song, ..TIM: Yes, the one that wasn't actually....it's had a very strange ory because Andrew wrote the tune a long, long time ago and ially, it was called Saladin Days which was an atrocious pun based

Teaching on Prayer.

"But by the end of the evening it became clear to me that what I had been watching (whatever the views or convictions of the young English authors, Tim Rice and Andrew Lloyd Webber) was a highly professional secular fancy-dress melodrama based on the pressures surrounding a pop idol on the wane, nerve-wracked and exhausted by the demands made by his fans."

—Rosemary Say
'The Sunday Telegraph'

'SUPERSTAR' SPEAKS:

You were quoted in a recent issue of Rolling Stone as saying, while on to in the Philippines, that you are bigger than the Beatles. Were you really serious when you said that?

Like, I didn't really mean I was bigger than the Beatles, I mean like at thi point in history, I mean more to the kids than the Beatles, sell more records. That's all I meant. I could never be really bigger than them.

But when you said that, there was a widespread reaction to it. Promoters regused to book you, certain radio stations wouldn't play your records, ministe claimed you had upset the Christian background of rock and roll.

There are a lot of Phillistines in the Philippines, man. I didn't mean anyth disrespectful about it, I didn't mean to offend all those people. But it's a matte of record that more people throughout the world celebrate the 25th of Decemb than the 5th of November.

A lot of people want to know if you're ever bugged by having such a fam father. Do you feel like you have some pretty large shoes to fill? Does it ever ge you down?

It used to, man, it used to. Like I used to be jealous of all the things He could do. Like the creation of the Universe was heavy, man, heavy. But as I gre older I realized that creation on such a large scale wasn't really my trip, that I could work some miracles of my own, such as healing the sick. I'm still a devel ing artist, you know, and I haven't begun to reach my potential yet.

Do you get along with your father?

I know there are many feuds in show business families, but I think the relationship between Him and me is basically a good one. Of course we have ou

round....um....Saladin who was a rather violent cove who hung arou in the Middle East when Richard the Lion Heart was on his crusa and we'd written a thing that never really got anywhere based Richard the Lion Heart and this tune was in it and it was a....ANDRE

Parable of the Friend at Midnight.

differences—in the way we dress, the length of our hair, politics, drugs—you know, the usual differences they call the "Generation Gap." But we can still sit down and talk about our differences openly. I think that's a good thing.

You've appeared at a large number of festivals—you always seem to draw crowds wherever you go. Do you remember some of the things that happened to you?

Yeah. I remember one festival that was run very bad. Like there weren't any proper health or sanitary facilities. On the second day the food ran out. All they had left were two fuckin' fishes and five fuckin' loeaves of bread. So I copped an "I Dream Of Jeannie" and fed the entire crowd of 150,000.

How did you do it? It must have been a miracle.

It sure was, man. Not even My Old Man could divide two anaemic herring 50,000 ways. So I used mass hypnosis—made them believe they had just eaten. Did you ever read "Mandrake the Magician?"

No, I missed that one.

Then at another festival, I pulled a bona fide miracle. Everybody was drinking water—that's all there was and everybody was down. I mean even Sly couldn't get them off their asses. So I changed the water into wine and everybody got stoned.

What kind of wine did you turn it into?

Well, pretty cheap wine. I don't have the trick down pat yet. Most of it was "Ripple" or "Twister." But I keep practising. That's the only way to be creative. You've got to have the technique down first.

There have been a lot of stories, some probably apocryphal, that you've done a lot of healing at these festivals.

Well, at some festivals there was some bad acid going around—rat poison, you know. Lots of people were freaking out. So I got up on stage and calmed the crowd down, told a few jokes—even did an acoustic number with a guitar—and a lot of people who had been freaking out were calmed down again. Some of them had been pretty bad—they thought they were blind, or crippled, or leprosy was eating them up. Pretty far out.

Considering what happened at festivals last year, do you foresee any more happening this year?

I do, but they're gonna have to be on a much smaller scale. Well-regulated and well-run. Some of them were so big that I felt that even I couldn't control the crowd.

Will you be performing at any more festivals?

I've become pretty disillusioned about the whole thing. I've been on the road for a few years now and I'd like to spend more time at my home in Woodstock with Mary, and make things. I'm really into carpentry, you know, I love

for school children....FROST: For school children? Yes, can we hear a bit of that, that was....this was....TIM: It's the same tune exactly.... ....and it just....um....I mean, it just went, instead of 'Oh so he was a christ', it was 'Those were the days, good old Saladin days'....that sort

Warning against Covetousness.

working with my hands and building things. I'm building all the furniture for our home. I'm also building a cabin on our land—I'm very close to the earth, you know, Capricorn.

I was wondering what you were . . . You and Mary have been together for several years. Are you going to be getting married, do you believe in that sort of social tie, you know, in the whole philosophy of marriage as a form of individual expression?

I don't really believe in marriage. Mary and I don't need a piece of paper to tell us we're in love, right, hon (Magdalene smiles and nods affirmatively). But if we ever decide to have children, we would get married for their sake.

It's been said that you have more groupies than any other star. Does that bother you, Mary?

MM: Not really. Jesus and I have an understanding about such things. I'm only interested in his happiness and I know that he loves me, no matter what happens.

Jesus, I was wondering what your own early influences were. Was there a lot of music in your home?

No, but there was a lot of donkey shit; I was born in a manger (laughs). Seriously, though, there was always some kind of music around, either my mother singing a lullabye, a passing shepherd playing on his pipes, or those damn angels with their damn harps. Everytime I would be falling out, I'd be awakened by a beam of light and angels singing. I hardly ever got to sleep with all that music. My father's record collection, too.

Which particular artists impressed you?

Oh, there are so many I can't begin to name them. Everything in your life is an influence, you know.

How about a few names.

Oh, all right. Well, let's see, Moses, Buddah, Mohammed, Lao Tzu, Bernie Taupin, Bennie Maupin, Charley Patton, General Patton, Robert Johnson, Lynd? Johnson, Jackie Gleason, Ralph Gleason, Smokey Robinson, Robinson Crusoe, Enrico Caruso, Vaughn Monroe, Bill Monroe, Ed Roebuck, Sears and Roebuck, Sears and Crofts, Seals and Crofts, Jim and Jean, Bunky and Jake, Bunky and Ann Marie, Anne Murray, Fra Filippo Lippi, Leo "The Lip" Durocher, Leo the Lion, Jimmy Lyons, Dick Tiger, Steve Katz, Octave Maus, Max Roach, Spyder Turner, Tina Turner, Tina Louise, Louisa May Alcott, May Britt, Britt Eckland, Elton Britt, Elton John, John Stewart, Stewart Granger, Wayne Granger, Chuck Wayne, Ray Chuck, Ray Charles, Charles Brown, Brownie McGhee, Gale McGhe? Gale Storm, Gorilla Monsoon, Haystacks Calhoun, Haystacks Balboa, Ferdinand Megellan, Love the Magician, Mike Love , Sonny Dove, Sonny Til, Sunny Murra? Arthur Murray, Arthur Lee, Lee Dotson, Lee Hazelwood, Matt Hazeltine, Matt

of thing, I mean....(laughter)....and various other sort of....ANDRE?
I can't really remember what those lines were now. TIM: That show h?
other lyrics which um, you know, because the tunes, two or three of t?
tunes, not very many were almost something else. Then we entered th?

Parable of the Rich Fool.

Goukas, Matt "Guitar" Murphy, George Murphy, Lowell George, Lowell Fulsom. . .
get the idea?

Yes, I think so. You had many influences.

I almost forgot Delta Blues—they're a couple of black blues singers I met last year down south—Peg Leg Delta and Blind Willie Blues.

What part of the south are they from?

They're from Mississippi, man. All those old blues singers are from Mississippi, aren't they?

I think so. What were your first gigs?

I started out playing rhythm guitar for the Carpenters. Then like everyone else played in John Mayall's Bluesbreakers. I gigged around L.A. for a while—Tuesday nights at the Troubador, the whole thing, you know. Then I came to New York and here I am.

You're making a lot of money now. What are you doing with it?

Now that I'm successful, I don't intend to let it get to me. My manager Judas takes 30 pieces of silver per show and invests the rest back into the community. I'm planning to start my own label soon. I've already got a 16-track studio in my log cabin at Woodstock. Just a simple little 16-track studio in the woods—no fancy furniture or carpeting—just $300,000 worth of rustic recording equipment.

You've been involved with a lot of famous supersessions, such as the time you played with the entire Roman army. Are you planning to do any more of that?

As a matter of fact I'm jamming with Jimi and Janis tomorrow. Jimi has switched to harp, you know. You should hear him—unbelievable. He's driving everybody crazy up there—they're used to Mozart and Debussy and Elmer Bernstein.

That's a nice robe you're wearing. Where did you get it?

Thanks a lot. Mary made it for me. It's really my formal robe—you know, for weddings, bar mitzvahs, crucifixions—I don't usually wear it around the house.

How about drugs?

As you probably know I was into a heavy drug trip for a while. I took a lot of acid, I kept seeing God, even though my father wasn't within a thousand miles of me. I tried everything, including scag. It all ended up in a real bad bummer I had at Woodstock. Some of us were sitting in a circle and talking—there was Mick, Bob, John, George and Al Aronowitz—talking and dropping acid. All of a sudden I had a vision that I was on a stage in the middle of a race track and there were 300,000 people watching me being nailed to a cross. I never took another trip after that. I'm not too stable to begin with, even though I was born in one. You know I twice committed myself to mental institutions. . .

ne for the Eurovision Song Contest under the title 'Try it and See', as sort of knees-up, um, sort of 'Boom Bang-a-Bang' type record and it was rejected and it was....you know, we still thought it was a good hastly tune....FROST: Good, ghastly tune....very terrible....as good....

Teaching on Watchfulness.

Have you finished your next album yet?

Yes, I just finished it last week. It's a live album called "Jesus Christ Live i the Garden of Gethsemane." It's just live recordings of all my hits.

I didn't know you played the Garden..

Yeah, I played it on my last tour. My next three albums are "Jesus Christ' Greatest Hits," "The Best of Jesus Christ," and "The Jesus Christ Story." There' a lot of unreleased material but the record company is sitting on it. They'll wait until I die before they releast it.

How about the movie of your recent tour?

They finished it but we haven't decided on a name yet. Some of the possibilities are "Gimme Barabas," "Mount Olive Pop," and "Mad Dogs and Isrealites." There's a great scene near the end called The Last Press Party which takes place at Max's Kansas City. Just fabulous.

Sounds great. I'd like to get into your lyrics for a moment. In one of you songs you say, "It is finished." What did you mean by that?

The dream is over. What more can I say?

How about the line, "Arise and take up they bed." Are you advocating fr love?

Heterosexual love, yes. But in another song I say to a man, "Come out of the man, thou unclean spirit."

Are you aware of those four self-proclaimed Jesusologists, Matthew, Marl Luke and John, who go around analyzing every word you say and collect your garbage? Have you heard of the Jesus Archives and the Jesus Liberation Front, otherwise known as Christianity?

I've never met the four gentlemen, but I think their interpretations of my lyrics as a masterplan to save mankind are the mad musings of four paranoid minds. I'm just a simple country boy singin' about what I know best—horses, donkeys, sheep, good guys, outlaws, the good life. How much are these guys gonna make out of me when they publish their books? I wish they'd leave me and my garbage alone.

Do you have any long-range goals?

Yes. I'd like to live on my farm and make love with Mary Magdalene and play music and live to a ripe old age. But with guys like you following me arou and bugging me, balling me, dissecting my lyrics, treating me like some kind of god, you'll probably drive me to an early grave. But as the song says, "You can' keep a good man down . . ."

Judas: I hate to interrupt, but Jesus has a very busy schedule tonight.
That's alright. I think I have enough here anyway.

—'Rock' Magazir

ANDREW: We thought we'd put it in, I mean, it was always very **FROST:** So you gave it to King Herod. **ANDREW:** Yes we gave it King Herod because we thought that King Herod really would do th sort of thing, because he was just sort of just such a horrible guy. H

Devotion to Duty.

US
udas—must you betray me with a kiss?

ER
Vhat's the buzz? Tell me what's happening

ER AND APOSTLES
Vhat's the buzz? Tell me what's happening
lang on Lord we're gonna fight for you

US
ut away your sword
on't you know that it's all over?
: was nice but now it's gone
Vhy are you obsessed with fighting?
tick to fishing from now on

WD
ell me Christ how you feel tonight
Do you plan to put up a fight?
Do you feel that you've had the breaks?
Vhat would you say were your big mistakes?
o you think that you may retire?
Did you think you would get much higher?
Iow do you view your coming trial?
ave your men proved at all worthwhile?

ome with us to see Caiaphas
You'll just love the High Priest's house
ou'll just love seeing Caiaphas
ou'll just die in the High Priest's house
ome on God this is not like you
et us know what you're gonna do
ou know what your supporters feel

'Show me a miracle' and that's....uh....what it says in the Bible really.
OST: How....how about writing for Jesus, I mean, writing somgs for
us....Was that the most difficult thing to do? TIM: Yes, I think it....,
hink it probably....probably was....FROST: Gethsemane had a

Two Calamities.

You'll escape in the final reel
Tell me Christ how you feel tonight
Do you plan to put up a fight?
Do you feel that you've had the breaks?
What would you say were your big mistakes?

Come with us to see Caiaphas
You'll just love the High Priest's house
You'll just love seeing Caiaphas
You'll just die in the High Priest's house

Now we have him! Now we have got him!

CAIAPHAS

Jesus you must realise the serious charges facing you
You say you're the Son of God in all your handouts—
    well is it true?

JESUS

That's what you say—you say that I am

ANNAS

There you have it gentlemen—
    what more evidence do we need?
Judas thank you for the victim—
    stay a while and you'll see it bleed!

CROWD

Now we have him! Now we have got him!
Take him to Pilate!

PETER'S DENIAL

MAID BY THE FIRE

I think I've seen you somewhere—I remember
You were with that man they took away
I recognise your face

completely different middle note, didn't it? ANDREW: Yes which
had....TIM: I've forgotten how that went too. FROST: When you
for instance, that to you the music of....was Geth....in a way the lyr
last part of Gethsemane, what did you mean by that? ANDREW:

The Lesson to be learnt from them.

Jésus-Christ
uper star »
opéra rock
nglais, sera
réé à Paris

'EST une petite bonne
femme aux yeux paille
à qui rien ni personne
'siste : Annie Fargue.

l'histoire d'un opéra rock
quel les Américains se di-
'rgue après avoir porté à

trice de « Oh ! Calcutta » la
pièce la plus érotique et la plus
nue que l'on ait jamais vue, s'at-
taque maintenant à « Jésus-
Christ ». Et pourquoi pas ?

En janvier 1971, un de ses
amis Américains lui apporte un
double 33 tours étrange. Couver-
ture jaune sur laquelle est écrit
« Jésus-Christ super star ».
Opéra rock lyrique de Tim

Centro Culturale
San Fedele
20121 Milano - Piazza S. Fedele 4
Tel. 80-94-81

MCA Records - Italy
20121 Milano - Galleria del Corso 4
Tel. 79-07-46

dibattito su

Jesus Christ
Superstar

Opera rock

interverranno gli autori
Andrew Lloyd Webber e Tim Rice

Martedì 1 Dicembre 1970
ore 21,15
Auditorium San Fedele - Via Hoepli 3/5

Il presente invito è valido per Lei e per coloro
ai quali desidera estenderlo.

a shocking pianist, but when he's doing... (plays piano) the orchestra
the rock group go into unison and the....the....the rock group plays
sort of line and the orchestra....instead of having an orchestration is
ually in unison, I mean it's doing all this sort of (plays piano)....all in

Healing of the Infirm Woman.

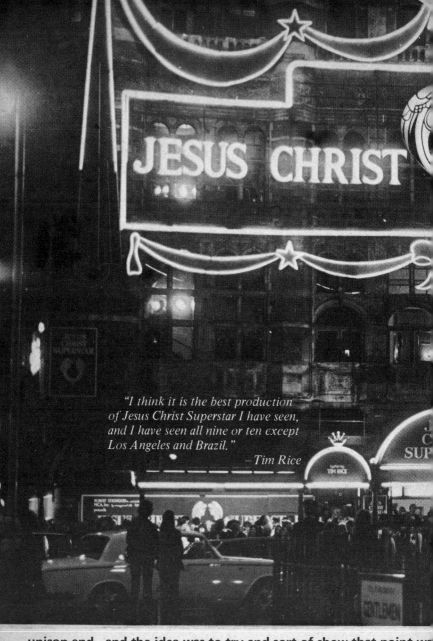

> *"I think it is the best production of Jesus Christ Superstar I have seen, and I have seen all nine or ten except Los Angeles and Brazil."*
>
> — *Tim Rice*

unison and...and the idea was to try and sort of show that point wa
fusing of the elements and everything together and I think a
number of musical themes that run through the piece that are
actually sung or anything that recur in various ways. At the end....a

Journey through Peræa.

f the first act and the end of the opera and the end of the overture
d in the same way. I think, if I remember rightly, how it goes....
s piano)....the things in it and the idea behind Gethsem....the last
e of Gethsemane at the end, which we call John 19:41, I think

A message to Herod.

SUPER

Pop go
—so inr

"A prophet is still not without honour except in his own country"

JESUS
is
the
TRUE

JESUS
is
RISEN
and
LIVE

ROCK JE

DEMO

has been missed by virtually everybody, funnily enough, which is
very thing....(piano)....you've got this sort of heavily over-romantic
(piano)....writing....(piano music)....what on earth was that doing at
end of this rock music....anything....but they missed the point of it

Healing of the Dropsical Man.

K—BUT IT'S NOT THE REAL SUPERSTAR

SS Thursday August

esu

ently!

Daily Mail, Thursday, August 10, 1972

t's big first night

, mawkish...electronic gospel

ot for me!

BY PETER LEWIS

Superstar is presented as no more than a man—the Resurrection is not even hinted at.

The only dramatic significance the show attempts arises from the fascinating question why . . .

ter. Lyrics
music by
ober. Poloce

matters at
ght as well
ow I have
hole concep-
Christ Super-
my nostrils.

The ladies' banners and leaflets stated that J. C. Superstar was not their Jesus and that the show misrepresented their beliefs.

As it turned out, the show does not represent any religious beliefs at all. It is a pageant-concert of amplified beat numbers strung round the last seven days in Jerusa-

old hat. Its strongest asset is the set, a black arena in which light can be excitingly employed

Mastes
Fro
could
cause

PARIS 22-2708 or 2

LONDON 01-353 8

lion by Jim
th borrow-
orus lines
into the

Hun
Gar

A b
Gary B
home B
Notting
dens, wit
Leed
helped t
the nu

'Sing a hymn' demo at Jesus show

BY DAVID WIGG

az tars ran
n-slinging
rrived

Ho

Police
in
16-year-
holiday
One o
Gronn n
hospital

The
Conco
quieter
the
engines

The Daily Telegraph, Thursday, August 10, 1972

First Night

'Superstar' startlin and nauseating

JOHN BARBER

se it was written as a sort of rather a Straussian....Richard Straussian
d of...not exactly a sort of satire was the wrong word, but a sort of...
tly sort of....irony to the horror of this Crucifixion at which this
is being killed in a ghastly way as a sort of sacchariney kind of two

Three Parables of Feasting

Stephen Tate and angels

Photograph by Donal

Little here for card-carrying Christians

Jesus Christ Superstar
Palace

Irving Wardle

Loaded with all the gifts of Mammon, plus a mass-circulation blessing from the Bishop of Southwark, *Jesus Christ Superstar* finally arrives in its homeland. Stifling memories of *The Maid of the Mountains*, which lately graced the same stage, we can point to the international productions and record sales (over four million) and stop apologizing for the British musical. The Second Coming itself could not have aroused more tumult than broke out last night among the £2.50 stalls patrons.

There are plenty of stylistic things to commend in the show. What offsets them is the widespread assumption, possibly shared by the authors Andrew Lloyd Webber and Tim Rice, that it has something to do with Christianity. For card-carrying Christians any youthful interest in the gospel is automatically seized as evidence of a

great new awakening; but how they can adduce it from this piece, compared with which the Californian Jesus-freaks seem like stylites, defeats understanding.

Tracing the events from the entry into Jerusalem to the Crucifixion, the action is presented from the viewpoint of Judas Iscariot. He starts by reminding Jesus of the past ("No talk of God then—we called you a man") and warning him that the movement will be suppressed if it gets out of hand. To this sensible advice Jesus responds with hysterical anger, flopping into the Magdalene's lap to be soothed and annointed, again to Judas's disgust (" people who are starving matter more than your feet and hair.")

Jesus, as he repeatedly confesses, is tired of it all ; and apart from one shrill scream which clears out the temple, his role throughout is passive. " Heal yourselves " he advises the cripples who are clawing at him ; he has no parable (or, indeed, any Biblical dialogue) and his silence before Herod and Pilate suggests exhaustion

What remains, of course, are the

events and the name ; both of which are Box Office. To these the authors have added the modern pop fable—projecting the image of a declining star, first idolized and then torn apart by the fickle ravers, on to the wide screen of Christian myth. The only question is that of underlying intention. Starting as a humanist criticism of Christ, the show becomes intoxicated with the events themselves as soon as Judas's prophesy starts coming true; and whatever the appeal of its second half, it is not to the mind.

At which point we arrive at the question of style. The most important and welcome innovation is that the authors have entirely dispensed with a book—notoriously the weakest element in modern musicals. The piece is scored throughout, sometimes dropping into near-recitative, but mostly blasting out big numbers which gradually induce a state of possession. Lyrics and music alike obey a principle of fragmentation. Even separate words are sometimes smashed into individual nonsense syllables, while Mr Webber's

score is mainly built from three and four note phrases repeated over elaborately instrumented but rhythmically obsessive accompaniments. The effect is like switched-on Carl Orff; and it is mindstunning.

Add to that the spectacle of a Jerusalem fit to be visited by Dr Who: a raked unit containing two orchestra pits (in addition to the theatre's own pit), inset with portholes through which guards appear with dazzling silver shields, and temple merchants with huge interlocking cogwheels. Flimsy opaque pillars shiver down from above, and Pilate washes his hands in a perspex hour-glass. Brian Thomson's designs are most sophisticated S-F inventions, and they score many individual points; as where the arrested Jesus is surrounded by journalists with fantastic cameras, and where Herod (Paul Jabara) is swept on, buried in concubines, on a vast silver inflatable to deliver a show-stopping *dolce vita* challenge to his prisoner. (" Prove to me that you're no fool/Walk across my swimming pool.') But again, like the writing, the sets are calcu-

lated to glamourize and [...] the sense of the events [...] ciple of brutal yet dehum [...] petition is summed up to [...] end where Pilate admir [...] strokes of the lash with [...] phone lead.

Of Jim Sharman's cast, their voices are trained [...] stand the savage dema[...] on them. Paul Nicholas, a[...] Hunt Jesus with an aub[...] and delicate fastidiou[...] has to push his voice i[...] ordinary falsetto roars w[...] him husky and vague on [...] in gentler passages.

Stephen Tate's Judas, most electrifying performa[...] exceeds him in sheer [...] sound; the difference b[...] that Mr Tate's playing spe[...] a passionate convictio[...] originally leads one to t[...] show more seriously than[...] quently deserves. For [...] pleasure, the honours go[...] Gillespie's Magdalenc [...] torch performance, sun[...] fully and carrying an un[...] of irony which one wishe[...] the chance to develop.

lambs and sort of the good shepherd image of Christ that has, I t

you know, been so lumbered on young people, it certainly was on

TIM: Right....ANDREW: When I was at school....FROST: What wa

toughest thing....toughest thing to write words-wise, Tim? Jesus a

The Three Parables of Divine Compassion.

MILTON SHULMAN

THERE ARE certain theatrical events that are bound to defy the impact of criticism and Jesus Christ Superstar at the Palace is one of them.

Already a super smash-hit —in spite of cool notices in New York—it has by now received almost as much publicity as the Second Coming itself.

With sheep-like queues clamouring to get in, and scalpers waxing rich outside its doors, a critic realises that what he has to say about this phenomenon is purely of academic rather than financial interest.

Why, he must ask himself, should anyone want to see it? It is a hit and, of course, some limited social prestige accrues to anyone who has seen a hit.

It is a best-selling record and those who know the songs will want to see the dramatic justification for the tunes that have been haunting them.

I suspect, however, that it will not be the pop or rock enthusiasts that will keep this show running but sincere Christian porpagandists who have convinced themselves that this sort of rhythmic evangelism—discotheque Billy Graham—is just the thing to bring the young back to the Church.

This Bishop of Southwark, for example, found in it the "explosive message of Jesus." On the other hand, Peter Hall, the theatre director, thought that it said "nothing about Christ and nothing for or against religion."

My own view is that it is only on the most naive and vulgar level that Jesus Christ Superstar can be said to approach anything like a valid religious experience.

The musical's Christ-figure, constantly bathed in a silvery glow and wearing a robe so spotlessly white it could be a testimonial for a Biblical detergent called Jeez, is a symbol in the tradition of the palatable knick-knacks sold in the bazaars of Lourdes to commemorate the agony of Christ.

Jim Sharman's production, although it is apparently less spectacular than Tom O'Horgan's in New York, is still replete with enough gorgeous colours, divine costumes and extravagant choreography to justify the view that the Gospels were interpreted by Dior, Disney and Busby Berkeley.

An unfortunate touch, which ought immediately to be corrected, is the spurting of blood from Christ's body on the Cross. The crucifixion is no time to provoke hysterical giggles in the audience.

Indeed, Christ himself although played with handsome dignity by Paul Nicholas, is a curiously negative figure. It would need very little revision of music, lyrics and direction to turn this into a show about Mick Jagger or Georgie Best.

Ecstatic

The measure of its religious appeal can be judged by the fact that last night King Herod's Song—an irrelevant camp pastiche of a 1920's jazz number— received the most ecstatic reception.

In a way, it is a pity that the validity of its Christian theme tends to swamp any critical assessment of this musical.

On a less profound level, it has much to commend it. Its operatic form is a daring innovation in this rarely adventurous field.

Andrew Lloyd Webber's music has vitality and an enchanting tunefulness. Tim Rice's lyrics intelligently blend the language of the Bible and pop jargon without sounding forced or ludicrous.

As a rock opera, Superstar is never boring and is often stimulating. I only wish it had been about somebody else.

M: Yes, actually, funnily enough, Gethsemane itself was fairly quick.. ....that took about an hour or two hours, but 'I don't know how to ve Him' was a very tough one....um....if you....if you've got a really ong melody (a) it's a challenge to try and do justice to it and...and (b)

The Unjust Steward.

Superstar subdued

IN THE Broadway production of **Jesus Christ Superstar** they buried the whole huge orchestra and rock group beneath the stage and then proceeded to bombard the audience with the music through banked amplifiers. In the spacious Mark Hellinger Theater it worked. The singing and the score sounded marvellously extravagant, matching the explosion - a - minute overblown production the show was given.

In the London show, the rock musicians sit pointlessly on each side of the stage, which cuts almost in half the area for Cecil B. de Mille-style action by actors and singers. The musical strength compared with New York is in roughly (and sadly) the same proportion. At the Palace, the backing trio and chorus for the title song were so fragile that "Superstar" lost much of its stupendous dramatic impact.

So, all right, this is an underplayed production compared with its transatlantic predecessor (which, certainly, went over the top on occasions) and, one gathers, is very deliberately so. mistakenly in my view, however. It says volumes for the magnificently apt and modern writing of Andrew Lloyd Webber and Tim Rice that the music still comes through the mists.

As well as the title song, " I Don't Know How to Love Him," " Everything's Alright " and " Could We Start Again, Please " are confirmed as fine pieces—and just listen to the sharp countersinging humorously, set against the crowd crying snatches of " Superstar " in the street.

Those who laugh at the high-camp of " King Herod's Song " (done sort of Jolson-with-cuties style) will perhaps scarcely believe that it is low-camp compared with the Broadway treatment, even though no concubine's nipples were evident in the Mark Hellinger as they were (accidentally?) at the Palace.

The musical success of London's " Superstar "—still *the* rock opera so far, with only " Catch My Soul " and the different-in-intent " Tommy " in the same league—is undoubtedly Dana Gillespie as Mary Magdalene: a warm soul voice seizing the good songs she's given. John Parker (Pilate) and Richard Barnes (Peter) take their singing chances, too. I fear, however, that so far the Jesus of Paul Nicholas is no more than adequate and that, after Ben Vereen's blues-loaded passion on Broadway, the Judas of Stephen Tate is thin.

The singing and the playing generally need more spunk and there's no reason why more work and less uptightness shouldn't generate it.

Derek Jewell

you can't play around um....with the syllables too much, I mean....u
you, you....it's almost like doing a very hard crossword puzzle, eve
thing has to fit exactly....FROST: Yes....TIM: You know the son
found the easiest, I can churn off sort of rather....um....you know

Dives.

u've got the wrong man lady I don't know him
And I wasn't where he was tonight—never near the place

DIER
That's strange for I am sure I saw you with him
You were right by his side and yet you denied—

ER
I tell you I was never ever with him

O MAN
But I saw you too—it looked just like you

ER
I don't know him!

RY MAGDALENE
Peter—don't you know what you have said
You've gone and cut him dead

ER
I had to do it don't you see?
Or else they'd go for me

RY MAGDALENE
It's what he told us you would do—
I wonder how he knew ...

PILATE AND CHRIST
Friday

ATE

Who is this broken man cluttering up my hallway?
Who is this unfortunate?

DIER
Someone Christ—King of the Jews

ppant lyrics very quickly but um....FROST: So when it comes down
simple short words....TIM: And also try to....I mean....I find it a little
t tricky to identify with a, you know, female....um....loose lady, you
ow, um....I....I put myself in a position that I hadn't been in before,

Lazarus.

Oh so this is Jesus Christ, I am really quite surprised
You look so small—not a king at all
We all know that you are news—but are you king?
  King of the Jews?

JESUS
  That's what you say

PILATE
  What do you mean by that?
  That is not an answer
  You're deep in trouble friend—
  Someone Christ—King of the Jews
  How can someone in your state be so cool about your fate?
  An amazing thing—this silent king
  Since you come from Galilee then you need not come to me
  You're Herod's race! You're Herod's case!

MOB
  Ho-ho Sanna Hey Sanna Sanna Sanna Ho
  Sanna Hey Sanna Ho and how
  Hey JC, JC please explain to me
  You had everything where is it now?

KING HEROD'S SONG

HEROD

Jesus I am overjoyed to meet you face to face
  You've been getting quite a name all around the place
  Healing cripples raising from the dead
  And now I understand you're God at least
    that's what you've said

you know, you know, for that one and tried to think how I wou
react in that position which is....which is a little bit difficult. FROST
Fascinating. We'd better take a break there, when we come back, we
be talking in addition with some of the critics of Jesus Christ Sup

The Raising of Lazarus.

ENTER THE FIRST ANNUAL

MR. JESUS CHRIST CONTEST

presented by the

THE FIRST NATIONAL CHURCH OF THE EXQUISITE PANIC, INC.
ROBERT DELFORD BROWN, FOUNDER, LEADER, and PRESIDENT

● ●

THE EVENT WILL TAKE PLACE THURSDAY MARCH 30 at MIDNIGHT

at the

GARRICK THEATRE   152 BLEECKER STREET   NEW YORK CITY

● ●

CONTESTANTS WILL BE REQUIRED
TO POSE FOR 30 SECONDS BEFORE A GARLANDED STYROFOAM CROSS
WINNERS TO BE CHOSEN FOR ORIGINALITY, SPIRITUALITY, and TASTEFULNESS

● ●

A DISTINGUISHED PANEL OF JUDGES WILL AWARD THE FOLLOWING PRIZES:

1st PRIZE: A ONE-WAY TICKET TO JERUSALEM ON LUFTHANSA AIRLINES,
VIA FRANKFURT, GERMANY (based on group rates). Or cash equivalent.

2nd PRIZE: SIX BEAUTIFUL ROSE BUSHES TO GROW YOUR OWN CROWN OF
THORNS. Or cash equivalent.

3rd PRIZE: A LOVELY SET OF HAMMER AND NAILS. Or cash equivalent.

● ●

ADMISSION TO SEE CONTEST OR TO BECOME A CONTESTANT $3.00

● ●

TO ENTER
SIMPLY PRINT YOUR NAME ON THE DOTTED LINE AND PRESENT THIS FORM
IN THE GARRICK THEATRE LOBBY AFTER YOU HAVE PURCHASED YOUR
TICKET THE NIGHT OF THE CONTEST.

all contestants will be required to sign a release form before the contest begins.

ar and the whole business of presenting Jesus at all on stage. We'll be
ck in just a moment.   FROST: Now it's our pleasure to
lcome to the stage one of the people who has reviewed Jesus Christ
per Star and we've got others with us who have had their doubts

Healing of the Ten Lepers.

about it, and so let discussion begin. Will you welcome back to o[
stage, Malcolm Boyd, the Reverend Malcolm Boyd....(clapping).
Thank you very much....Yvonne....Andrew....Tim....come and sit dow[
BOYD: It's nice to see you again. FROST: Very good to see you agai[

Christ blesses the Little Children.

alcolm, last time it was a Book Luncheon in Cleveland, I remember.
OYD: That's right. FROST: But the....what were your feelings about...
ut Jesus Christ Super Star? BOYD: I'm awfully glad you asked,
vid, because I've been looking at the show outside on the monitor

Healing of the Blind Man at Jericho

Welcome to ROLLING STONE'S Journalism Corner. Our subject this iss
is How to Conduct a Telephone Interview, and the example has been kindly pr
vided by Jon Stewart, a San Francisco writer:

Hello, Bureau of Information and Publicity. Douglas Benton.

Mr. Benton. My name is Jon Stewart and I'm calling from San Francisco.
I'm trying to run down more complete information on something that's presum
ably being built in Alabama called Holyland, USA. Can you help me with this?

Well, I'll give you everything I can. They're projecting a partial opening ir
late '73. Alton B. (Sonny) Hankins of Rosinton, Alabama, is one of the princip
in the company and the project will cost ten million dollars.

Ten million dollars. What kind of things will the project include?

OK. The theme of the park will be, of course, Holyland. There will be th
walled city of Jerusalem. But what they say they're starting construction on
first will be the Plan of Salvation Garden. At the entrance will be a statue of
Christ 110 feet tall. Fabricated of fiberglass and lighted. They're projecting a
parking lot for 10,000 cars.

My gosh.

A camper-trailer park and a three-hundred unit motor hotel called "The
Inn".

Just "The Inn".

"The Inn". Ah, inside—I'm quoting now—will be re-created in sound,
architecture, dress, crafts and many ancient Bible cities, including the Garden o
Eden, ancient Babylon, Phoenicia, Egypt, the desert areas, ancient Jerusalem,
Rome, Greece . . .

I . . . I don't understand. This is . . . those are . . . what are those things?

Ah, they're areas within the park. In other words—the way I understand
it now—say Egypt and the desert areas will be a camel ride to the miniature
pyramids.

And they'll **actually** have camels?

Yes—uh huh—and elephants.

And elephants.

There'll be a 15-acre lake called the Sea of Galilee. And there'll be slave
boat rides and Egyptian barge rides.

Slave boat rides.

And ah—let's see—you can be swallowed by the whale.

(Muffled laugh)—How they gonna do that?

Some kinda ride—a boatride into the lake and down into the whale.

Well—that's remarkable.

And there'll be a 12,000-seat amphitheatre—a replica of the Roman
Coliseum where they will hold chariot races and gladiator fights in the afternoo

and I see very attractive people doing songs from the album which
love and most of us do, and I wrote a very critical review that the N
York Times asked me to do and it wasn't about the album and it was
even about the road company. I happen to have been to the ro

Parable of the Pounds.

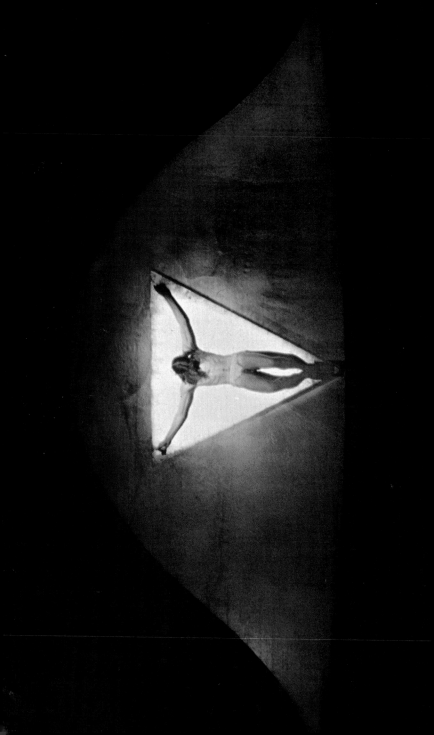

a passion play at night. Also, they will have Heaven and Hell.

Heaven and Hell.

The Wailing Wall, and you enter, according to the plans, through a time-
nel . . .

Through a time-tunnel.

That takes you back 2000 years.

Um-hum.

There'll be Roman shops, Grecian shops—a craftsman actually working, I
nk. All the rides are geared to the Biblical area and there'll be a Bible museum.
ey're supposed to be starting construction—moving the equipment in and doing
ne grading. I haven't been down recently so I don't know how far they've
ne. But they're hoping to have the Plan of Salvation Garden open to the
lic—which will be the only free part of it—by 1973. The statue of Christ
posedly will be visible five miles in either direction. It's comparable to a 13-
rey building.

A 13-storey building—yeah. Jesus. Is the state pretty excited about this?

Why, yes we are. Of course, anytime that anybody announces a major
raction, well—we get very excited about it.

Sure. Did Governor Wallace have any official comments about it?

Yes, he made the official announcement in conjunction with the Holyland
ple.

Well, it was pretty basic. He welcomed them to the state of Alabama and
gratulated them on their theme.

I see. Well, I thank you and I think I have all the information that I need
w.

Yes. They plan the opening and the official dedication on Palm Sunday of

Palm Sunday. Uh hum. Palm Sunday, '73. OK. Thanks a lot. Gotta ring
now.

Thank you for calling.

Bye.

Goodbye.

pany in New Haven, which was fine, it is Mr. O'Horgan's production
h I am criticising and I....(clapping) ...don't intend to sit here and
he heavy tonight, I'm not going to be the heavy, as if I'm sort of the
n guy or something, because I'm really not. I love your work and it

The Anointing at Bethany.

LIBERATOR

..."YOU SHALL KNOW THE TRUTH, AND THE TRUTH SHALL SET YOU FREE"

—JESUS

needs to be done properly and, as a matter of fact, someday I'd lov
be in on the staging, we ought to...it should be staged as a rock opera
the moment it's not....so many of us who care, I think our reactio
strong because we care in other words, I got the album, played it G

The Triumphal Entry.

FOR CHRIST'S SAKE, JOIN THE REVOLUTION!

COME NOW, ALL YOU RICH - WEEP AND
LAMENT BECAUSE MISERY IS COMING YOUR WAY - YOU
LIVE ON EARTH SO LAVISHLY, PLEASING YOURSELVES, BUT
YOU HAVE FATTENED YOUR HEARTS FOR THE SLAUGHTERING DAY.
JAMES 5:1-6

ay first and, you know, really liked it and there's so much in it that's
ery good, and I think the idea of not going on to the Resurrection is
, it's never bothered me in the least. Sex to me couldn't be vulgar
er almost any circumstances, only bad architecture could or some-

Withering of the Fig Tree.

"I first heard "Superstar", when I was in Yugoslavia filming "Fiddler on the Roof". An assistant of mine sent the record to me long before it was popular in America. I thought it to be pretentious but sincere work. The simplicity and sincerity that I found moved me deeply and I started to get all sorts of images, and I thought maybe it might be exciting to do a film without any spoken dialogue, maybe I can do an opera, maybe the connective tissue will be musical I didn't find it sacreligious, or the least bit offensive. I felt there was an effort these two young men to humanize Jesus rather than accent his divinity, but th leave a marvelous question at the end of the work. And without this question there wouldn't be any strength, I believe. in the Christian religion. Because it asks for faith, and without faith it would be nothing. I also liked the dramatic confrontation of characters so when I found out MCA had the rights I sent a letter to Lew Wasserman saying 'If you ever decide to make this into a motion picutre, I'd be interested in doing it.' Nothing happened for a while and then I got a phone call in Canada from Stigwood. We're going to shoot in in Israel — where else? It should be ready for release by Easter 1973. I don't plan to make as a period picture, I plan a timeless approach."

Norman Jewis
Film Directe

thing, I mean....(laughter)....you know what....there's something sexuality of Mr. O'Horgan's production....I'm not being sort of a sexual, I'm just saying I think a homosexual parody that's very anti movement right now and everything else, is very bad and I think t

Cleansing of the Temple.

you are the Christ you're the great Jesus Christ
ove to me that you're divine—change my water into wine
at's all you need do and I'll know it's all true
mon King of the Jews

sus you just won't believe the hit you've made round here
ou are all we talk about the wonder of the year
 what a pity if it's all a lie
ill I'm sure that you can rock the cynics if you try
 you are the Christ you're the great Jesus Christ
ove to me that you're no fool walk across
 my swimming pool
you do that for me then I'll let you go free
mon King of the Jews

nly ask things I'd ask any superstar
hat is it that you have got that puts you where you are?
m waiting yes I'm a captive fan
m dying to be shown that you are not just any man

 if you are the Christ yes the great Jesus Christ
ed my household with this bread—
 you can do it on your head
r has something gone wrong? Why do you take so long?
mon King of the Jews

ey! Aren't you scared of me Christ? Mr. Wonderful Christ!
ou're a joke you're not the Lord—
 you are nothing but a fraud
ake him away—he's got nothing to say!
et out you King of the Jews! Get out of my life!

a context in the show of vulgarity and by that I do not mean sex
 I just hope the movie, whoever he is, I wish they could take
erelli off of St. Francis and let him do it....FROST: Well Tim and
rew....BOYD: But I just wish that the movie could be from scratch

The Question as to Our Lord's Authority.

JUDAS' DEATH

JUDAS

My God! I saw him—he looked three-quarters dead!
And he was so bad I had to turn my head
You beat him so hard that he was bent and lame
And I know who everybody's gonna blame
I don't believe he knows I acted for our good

I'd save him all this suffering if I could
Don't believe... our good... save him... if I could

PRIEST 3

Cut the confessions forget the excuses
I don't understand why you're filled with remorse
All that you've said has come true with a vengeance
The mob turned against him—you backed the right hors

CAIAPHAS

What you have done will be the saving of Israel
You'll be remembered forever for this
And not only that you've been paid for your efforts
Pretty good wages for one little kiss

JUDAS

Christ! I know you can't hear me
But I only did what you wanted me to
Christ! I'd sell out the nation
For I have been saddled with the murder of you
I have been spattered with innocent blood
I shall be dragged through the slime and the mud
I have been spattered with innocent blood
I shall be dragged through the slime and the mud!

because this means a lot to a lot of people and it's got to be
properly and I'm sorry I'm the one tonight who has to say t
FROST: Well....BOYD: So many others have said it....TIM: I thin
understand that, may we just mention a point about the movie be

The Three Parables of Rejection.

3536 Madison Place N.G.
Minneapolis Minnesota
55418

Whom It May Concern:

ve recently bought one of your records "JESUS CHRIST SUPER-
AR"! wow! It was one of the most toughest records I ever bought!
1 15 and thought all religion was bunk! but after hearing this cool
rd, I feel more close to Jesus than I've ever felt before! I think it
ld make a great movie! Have you ever thought of it?

cefully yours,

e Schiminsky

Make more albums like that!

SUS IS COOL"

t two hours ago, we were talking with Norman Jewison who's
to direct the movie....FROST: Who has just done 'Fiddler on the
'....TIM: And he was saying that simplicity was the key, you
v....FROST: Yes. ANDREW: And there's one thing we're terribly

Three Questions of Temptation.

gratified about, he said there would not be one frame of the pic
that Tim and I and he won't have fully collaborated over and ag
which, for us, of course, is fantastic because it means that we wi
able to do what we like, but, can I just say one thing, I know in

Christ's own Question.

rk, everybody thinks 'Gosh, this is fantastic', you know, this....this
the New York thing, you know, this production is definitive and all
t, it isn't really, I mean, this is just the production in New York and
hoping that one day maybe, there will be other productions in New

Final Denunciation of the Jewish Leaders.

York, maybe by somebody else. I'm not knocking, as I like quite a ▶
of what Tom's done, but I think there are other ways of looking at it
BOYD: I don't and as a matter of fact, one of you said earlier that y◀
could see it done much more intimately. ANDREW: Yes. BOYD:

The Widow's Mites.

quite agree, as a matter of fact, I....I think the reason the Times possibly
[g]ot me into this at all is that for years, I've been reviewing quite a few
[fi]lms and so I was....it was always very interesting if there was a movie
[wi]th Jesus in it and I would kind of approach it with trepidation and

The Visit of the Greeks.

the Press Agent would meet me in the lobby of the theatre and s
please be kind and we would like to buy you dinner and I'd say 'No,
buy them all myself, thank you' and then I'd go back and either
would be the Jesus with the shaved armpits or it would be the a

The Prophetic Discourse on the Signs of the End.

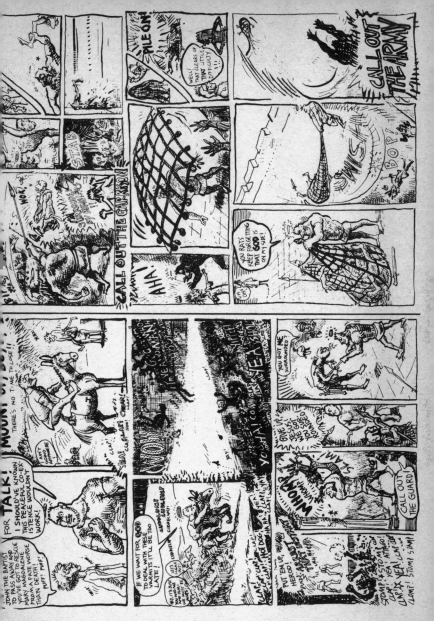

erican Jesus of George Stevens, Pasolini's was better except that was
activist Jesus who was angry all the time and I don't think Jesus was
er turning over the tables in the....in the temple all the time, nor
he forever a twenty-third psalm nice, he was a whole lot of things

The Three Last Parables of Judgment.

which you have seen and you have been discussing...TIM: Exact
ANDREW: You're absolutely right on... FROST: Let me put....let
put what you just said to some of the people in the front row he
Were your....I know we've got three or four more people in the fro

Judas' Treachery.

don't know how to love him.
don't know why he moves me
He's a man—he's just a man
He's not a king—he's just the same
As anyone I know
He scares me so
When he's cold and dead will he let me be?
Does he love me too? Does he care for me?
My mind is darkness now—My God I am sick I've been used
And you knew all the time
God! I'll never ever know why you chose me for your crime
For your foul bloody crime
You have murdered me! You have murdered me!

OIR
Poor old Judas
So long Judas

TRIAL BEFORE PILATE

(Including the 39 lashes)

PILATE

And so the king is once again my guest
And why is this? Was Herod unimpressed?

CAPHAS

We turn to Rome to sentence Nazareth
We have no law to put a man to death
We need him crucified—it's all you have to do
We need him crucified—it's all you have to do

PILATE
Talk to me Jesus Christ
You have been brought here—manacled, beaten

who had strong objections. Um....were your objections also based
the production or do you think this is something that shouldn't be
attempted at all? MAN: Based solely on the album, I in no case would
the production, I think the very concept of staging something about

Preparation for the Last Supper.

By your own people—do you have the first idea
    why you deserve it?
Listen, King of the Jews
Where is your kingdom?
Look at me—am I a Jew?

JESUS
    I have got no kingdom in this world—
        I'm through, through, through

MOB
    Talk to me Jesus Christ

JESUS
    There may be a kingdom for me somewhere—if I only knew

PILATE
    Then you're a king?

JESUS
    It's you that say I am
    I look for truth and find that I get damned

PILATE
    But what is truth? Is truth unchanging law?
    We both have truths—are mine the same as yours?

MOB
    Crucify him!

PILATE
    What do you mean? You'd crucify your king?

MOB
    We have no king but Caesar!

PILATE
    He's done no wrong—no not the slightest thing

Jesus, whose name is sacred to hundreds of millions of people, stag
it in a theatrical framework, I think is abhorrent, so I would in no c
see the production, I think the album itself is blasphemy enou
FROST: Why is the album blasphemy? MAN: Because it's not simpl

The Last Supper.

uestion that one tells half the truth about Jesus, namely that He is a
an, because one doesn't tell half the truth, to hundreds of millions of
hristians, He is the God Man and by merely presenting a humanity, a
ungling human person seeking his identity in the meaning of life, you

The Discourse of Comfort.

don't simply give one half to be completed in the next episode in ca
genius strikes again, you rather give a distortion, a blasphemy and I al
know that St. Paul himself said 'In the name of Jesus, every knee shou
bend, on earth, under the earth and in heaven', and here we have th

Promise of the Comforter.

sel idiocy and we have this loss of the sacred, and that's what's
ong with the entire public who think this topic is something to chat
out, and joke about and jest about. (Whistling from audience)....
YD: Could I say something here, I want....(clapping)....I feel that

The Agony in Gethsemane.

the sacred and the secular simply cannot be separated and I feel tha[t]
human life has an incredible holiness in it and I think that Jesus ca[n]
indeed by dramatised, can be seen on the stage. I also feel that we'[ve]
heard....as a matter of fact, I felt that Mr. O'Horgan could accuse me o[f]

The Arrest.

ething, if he wanted, as someone in the Church, because we have
ed so desperately in the Church to portray Jesus Christ to the world
lapping....that is the problem. He was human, not just plastic, you
holiness doesn't mean plastic, it includes the humaness, and I think

The Jewish Trials.

the sexual must be discussed and examined. FROST: Tim....TI
would just like to say in answer to....um....the criticism there th
Christ cannot be taken into the theatre, into the streets, into fields,
houses, then He has absolutely no meaning at all, I mean, I think J

Death of Judas.

GOD'S WORD

FUN
FAME
WANT
WASTE
FORTUNE
PLEASURE
WORRY
LOVE
POSSESSIONS
KNOCK
FAITH
GOD'S WILL
onder
PEACE
MPANIONS
SELF-RIGHTEOUSNESS
FOR OTHERS

st becomes one hundred thousand times more relevant if....if He can
r into everyday life. If He is only gettable at in an obscure church
n the end of the street, with lots and lots of ceremony, then that is
He has become meaningless. ANDREW: I remember....(clapping)....

The Roman Trial.

"Superstar" doesn't really make any point about anything. All it does is tell th story about the last seven days of Christ and points out the fact that to put it mildly he had a major effect on A — the people around him at the time and B everybody who's been around since and these are points which have been mad very well before by e.g. Matthew, Luke and John and several other noted writers. The only original thing about Superstar is that its the old story told in new way and if 'Superstar' has any message its to bring out the message to people who hadn't considered it."

Tim R

the Dean of St. Paul's and....in London saying 'Please', when we tal to him because, you know, we felt that we should discuss it with so one like that, he said, 'Please, try and take Jesus down off a stained window' and I....I think....I....I don't know whether we've succeede

Christ before Herod.

OB
We have no king but Caesar! Crucify him!

ILATE
He's done no wrong—no not the slightest thing

OB
We have no king but Caesar! Crucify him!

LATE
I see no reason—I find no evil
This man is harmless so why does he upset you?
He's just misguided—thinks he's important
But to keep you vultures happy I shall flog him

OB
Crucify him!

(Thirty nine lashes)

LATE
Where are you from Jesus? What do you want Jesus?
    Tell me
You've got to be careful—you could be dead soon—
    could well be
Why do you not speak when I have your life in my hands?
How can you stay quiet? I don't believe you understand

SUS
You have nothing in your hands
Any power you have comes to you from far beyond
Everything is fixed and you can't change it

LATE
You're a fool Jesus Christ—how can I help you?

oing that, but I certainly agree with Tim wholeheartedly, Jesus must
ave relevance today and if He can't be discussed on the David Frost
how in a serious manner, which I think we've been trying to do it, then
hat relevance has He....I'm sure He would....if He'd been alive, um....

Roman Trial Resumed.

MOB
    Pilate! Crucify him!
    Remember Caesar—you have a duty
    To keep the peace so crucify him!
    Remember Caesar—you'll be demoted, you'll be deported
    Crucify him!

PILATE
    Don't let me stop your great self-destruction
    Die if you want to you misguided martyr
    I wash my hands of your demolition
    Die if you want to you innocent puppet!

                        SUPERSTAR

VOICE OF JUDAS
    *E*verytime I look at you I don't understand
        Why you let the things you did get so out of hand
    You'd have managed better if you'd had it planned
    Why'd you choose such a backward time
        and such a strange land?
    If you'd come today you would have reached a whole natic
    Israel in 4 BC had no mass communication
    Don't you get me wrong—I only want to know

CHOIR
    Jesus Christ, Jesus Christ
    Who are you? What have you sacrificed?
    Jesus Christ Superstar
    Do you think you're what they say you are?

would have been very happy to have come and talked on the program
FROST: Let's round off our discussion of Jesus Christ SuperStar by ask
Yvonne to sing again the song that underlines what Tim and Andr
have been doing in stressing the humanity of Christ, whether one

Condemnation.

ell me what you think about your friends at the top
Who d'you think besides yourself's the pick of the crop?
uddah was he where it's at? Is he where you are?
Could Mahomet move a mountain or was that just PR?
Did you mean to die like that? Was that a mistake or
Did you know your messy death would be a record-breaker?
Don't you get me wrong—I only want to know

OIR
esus Christ Jesus Christ
Who are you? What have you sacrificed?
esus Christ Superstar
Do you think you're what they say you are?

THE CRUCIFIXION

SUS

od forgive them—they don't know what they're doing
Who is my mother? Where is my mother?
My God My God why have you forgotten me?
am thirsty
is finished
ather into your hands I commend my spirit

JOHN NINETEEN FORTY-ONE

ees with it or agrees with it, but in the universally acclaimed song 'I
n't know how to love Him' by the universally acclaimed Yvonne
iman. Would you sing that for us again....Thank you....(clapping)....
ank you very much indeed.

The Way to Calvary.

25 And there are also many other things which Jesus did, the which, if they should be written every one, I suppose that even the world itself could not contain the books that should be written. Amen.

ST. JOHN 21